Recapturing Technology for Education

Keeping Tomorrow in Today's Classrooms

Mark Gura
Bernard Percy

ScarecrowEducation
Lanham, Maryland • Toronto • Oxford
2005

Published in the United States of America
by ScarecrowEducation
An imprint of The Rowman & Littlefield Publishing Group, Inc.
4501 Forbes Boulevard, Suite 200, Lanham, Maryland 20706
www.scarecroweducation.com

PO Box 317
Oxford
OX2 9RU, UK

British Library Cataloguing in Publication Information Available

Library of Congress Cataloging-in-Publication Data

Gura, Mark.
  Recapturing technology for education : keeping tomorrow in today's
classrooms / Mark Gura, Bernard Percy.
     p. cm.
  Includes bibliographical references and index.
  ISBN 1-57886-109-8 (pbk. : alk. paper)
  1. Educational technology. 2. Education—Effect of technological
innovations on. I. Percy, Bernard. II. Title.

LB1028.3.G87 2005
371.33—dc22

                                        2004014668

⊗™ The paper used in this publication meets the minimum requirements of
American National Standard for Information Sciences—Permanence of
Paper for Printed Library Materials, ANSI/NISO Z39.48-1992.
Manufactured in the United States of America.

Contents

Introduction: Must Tomorrow Remain the Prisoner of Yesterday?

All truth passes through three stages: First it is Ridiculed. Second, it is Violently Opposed. Third, it is Accepted as being Self-Evident."

—Arthur Schopenhauer (1778–1860)

> Are teachers turning their backs on the new digital technologies? Without technology in the classroom, can our young people get the twenty-first century education they deserve?

TECHNOLOGY AND INTELLECTUAL WORK: UNQUESTIONED PARTNERSHIP EVERYWHERE, EXCEPT IN SCHOOL

Over the past two decades digital technologies have profoundly revolutionized intellectual work on planet earth. The emergence of two items have literally redefined the way people think, communicate, and work: the personal computer, an external extension of human intelligence that becomes increasingly cheaper, more portable, and more ubiquitous daily, and the World Wide Web, a multidimensional communications breakthrough that can put the entire human family on the same page nearly instantly.

These two innovations and a host of related technology items that support their use represent a vast step forward. Even casual contact with thought institutions such as libraries, businesses, news organizations, and governmental agencies reveals how much more gets done, and how greatly the quality of action and interaction can be expanded through the application of digital technologies.

One institution, ironically, remains largely unaffected—the institution most associated with the intellect and its training and growth—school. This is more than just unfortunate. It is outrageous! On the one hand, digital technologies have the potential to improve the teaching and learning process; they can be used by informed educators to motivate and instruct youngsters as never before. Technology can revitalize tired schools by offering a far broader platform of opportunities with which to engage students. Most significantly, it will engage them as residents of the new technology-shaped environment, satisfying a new need that has yet to be honestly acknowledged.

On the other hand, despite the broad-based acquisition of expensive computer hardware, networking, and Internet access; despite the expenditure of countless man hours in approaching the prospect of offering youngsters a technology-based facet of their school experience; despite much rhetoric, promise, and trial and failure attempts, *the potential for positive transformation that technology promises has not been realized. In truth, the effort to tap it has hardly begun in earnest.*

The reasons for the as yet-to-happen educational technology breakthrough are varied and it is worthwhile to reflect on and analyze them. Slamming the door on the technology and education connection at this point would risk giving up on the future before it has had an opportunity to present itself. Despite the protests of Philistines, Luddites, and hordes of unimaginative and lazy minds, technology remains poised as a platform to deliver the next significant phase in education. Human history is full of similarly slow, inelegant starts. Much waste and failure, for instance, preceded successful organ transplants before they began to redefine the state of human health care.

In his book *The Children's Machine*, educational technology pioneer Seymour Papert (1993) talks briefly about the groundbreaking work of the Wright brothers. Yes, he points out, we can say that Wilbur and Orville invented the heavier-than-air flying machine. And yet

the famous flyer made by Wilbur and Orville Wright did not prove itself by its performance. The duration of the best of several flights that day was only fifty-nine seconds! As a practical alternative to the horse-drawn wagon, it was laughable. Yet imaginative minds could see in it the birth of an industry that would lead to the jumbo jet and the space shuttle. Thinking about the future of education demands a similar labor of the imagination. The prevalent literal-minded, "what you see is what you get" approach measuring the effectiveness of computers in learning by the achievements in present-day classrooms makes it certain that tomorrow will always be the prisoner of yesterday. (p. 29)

The purpose of this book is to keep the educational technology discussion moving forward in a final push for the breakthrough that will surely follow. While many false starts have led to many dead ends, we have yet to come to the tipping point where the people who run our schools and classrooms have a clear understanding of what is possible with the technology and how to make it happen.

AT WHAT POINT ARE WE IN THE EVOLUTION OF A TECHNOLOGY-SUPPORTED EDUCATION?

In a sense, the experience of the New York City public schools is representative of what has happened. In the late 1990s, the people in charge of running the public schools in New York City began to receive quantities of worried feedback from parent groups and concerned citizens that the schools were out of step. There were few computers available to teachers and students. In our evolving information age this is not acceptable. In an extraordinary and gutsy move, the mayor and the school chancellor launched Project Smart Schools. Project Smart, as it came to be known, was a five-year $100 million-plus effort to almost overnight get the school system up to speed with technology.

After the equipment was purchased and installed, attention was finally turned to using it for education. Midstream in the project's first year, the responsibility for curriculum and instructional support and professional development was taken from the group who started the program, the system's Division of Management Information Services, a subsidiary of the operations part of the board of education. It was reassigned to the Division of Instructional Support, which overnight was charged with the training and support of roughly 25,000 teachers in approximately 400 schools. During the course of the project that charge was gradually expanded to all 80,000 teachers in all 1,200 schools. This was a great opportunity to observe on a mass scale the positive results and failures in one of the nation's first vast laboratories in the noble experiment of bringing technology to the classroom.

From the beginning of the program, though, word was out that the teachers simply weren't using the computers. It became an insider's joke that the computers were expensive paperweights that collected dust. This observation was seized on by those who continually argued that this oversized urban district was dysfunctional.

And it was true. In many instances the new director of the program, Mark Gura, saw it firsthand. His unit, the Office of Instructional Technology, went through all the obvious fixes: professional development, software acquisition, dissemination of best practices, experimentation with a variety of deployment models, and on and on. Interestingly, there were pockets, deep pockets, of successful use of the computers. Ironically, the schools experiencing success with the new classroom computers often were practically clones of the majority of schools in which computers were not put to good use. The reasons for success came down to understanding what was at stake, how computers could open up wonderful possibilities, sorting the techno-silliness from the deep veins of gold that lie beneath the surface, and knowing what to do to get on the right path.

For those of us who truly care about education—not the simpleminded perpetuation of the culture of traditional schooling, but the free-form possibility of human intellectual growth that "education" means in its pure sense—technology is no trendy trivial pursuit. Clearly the same technology that is revolutionizing the work of the intellect in all other institutions must be applied to education as well. The intellects of an entire generation, as well as the future of the institution of education, are at stake.

WHERE IS THE TRANSFORMATION HAPPENING?

Actually, bits and pieces of it are happening in almost every school in every district in our nation! The problem isn't that the vast numbers of schools and teachers out there aren't aware that technology-driven teaching and learning is happening in the world. The problem is that they see technology successes as curiosities, or as interesting examples, but ones that aren't tied to core, ubiquitous needs and educational dynamics.

Instructional technology is happening, but it's not happening systemically, not happening as a cultural shift, it hasn't happened as a chemical reaction, so to speak, and above all, we haven't seen the critical mass of understanding that will drive this change, regardless of budgets, politics, or conditions. In order for that to happen, people need to see that this change is extremely desirable, and it is eminently possible to bring about. This book will address those issues.

THE GOOD STUFF HAS YET TO COME

Years ago books like this one appeared and educators (like the authors of this book), who had logged years in the classroom and then as leaders, would wax poetic about the future use of the hard-to-come-by and wonderful-to-behold new computers for classrooms. They spoke about a future in which every teacher would have access to technology and the world would consequently be a wonderful place. The technology would literally redefine everything: what there was to be learned, how it could be taught, the logistics of running a classroom or a school, and on and on. It was easy to prognosticate great dreams in those days. Doing so was a low-stakes, no-risk game that attracted hoopla, felt good, and besides, who could say no to glowing predictions of a wonderful future? Unfortunately, it didn't work out that way.

Truth be told, technology hasn't turned the institution of education on its head. And because it hasn't, responsible folks, as well as relieved I-told-you-so-ers are singing a different song these days. Technology for education has, in large measure, missed its window of opportunity. The educational community, as well as the general public in the face of no easily picture framed miracles, or perhaps just too few of them, has come to an easy-to-draw, appealingly contrary conclusion that technology may not have a place in the classroom.

It's like Columbus and company turning back to Spain within spitting distance of the new world, Edison giving up on the lightbulb just three experiments short of the tungsten filament, the United States surrendering to Japan the week before Hiroshima. The use of technology for instruction has barely entered its maturity and educators who have witnessed the rise and fall of an endless parade of educational fads, whole language for example, are already writing it off as just one more boondoggle that turned out to have no value.

But education doesn't exist in a vacuum. All around it, in medicine, government, and business, technology continues to pay greater and greater dividends for professionals who have stayed the course. It can be so for technology in the institution of schooling too. It must!

THERE'S A BEAUTIFUL DIGITAL BABY IN THAT BATH WATER! (WELL, ACTUALLY IT'S ALREADY A DIGITAL TODDLER)

Instructional technology is no longer in its infancy. It is a field, a body of knowledge and practice, and a realm of experience that is steadily maturing. Accordingly, many ideas and notions associated with it have already been proven, discounted, or altered to reflect significant time and experience invested in them. It would be a great tragedy if the institution of education did not stay the course with something as powerful as this.

Education has honed for itself a dysfunctionally short attention span. We must resist the temptation to see instructional technology as just another in an interminable series of flavor-of-the-moment reform issues. Technology is not something to self-consciously do or think about. It is a series of high-intensity power tools that energize and empower everything we do naturally as learners and "knowers." As a result, we evolve new, more effective ways to learn, know, and communicate. We can't avoid technology, since it represents the logical, evolutionary next step for the human race to refine what it does with its intelligences. We can wisely embrace it and make our lives easier and more fruitful. Or we can deny the obvious and choose an uncomfortable roller-coaster ride as natural forces readjust themselves. As the traditional Chinese saying goes, It is easier to ride the horse in the direction it is going. Let us ride it well.

TWENTY-FIRST CENTURY TECHNOLOGY: BASIC EQUIPMENT FOR A TWENTY-FIRST CENTURY EDUCATION

Most areas of human intellectual activity have become so dependent on the support of digital technology that to offer our youngsters a school experience without it is to cheat them out of a vital aspect of their education. Why, then, are classrooms so slow to feature that technology as an essential engine to power teaching and learning?

Can you imagine a scientist working today who doesn't rely on computers and the Internet to gather data, process it, and report on findings and conclusions? A journalist, novelist, or technical writer who does not use a word processor or search the Web for source material? A mathematician who doesn't use computers to calculate and visualize the way numbers behave? All knowledge professionals today rely on technology. However, our schools represent a critical disconnect between the process of generating knowledge and that of acquiring it. While technology should currently be providing powerful support for teaching and learning, it remains, for the most part, an add-on, an enrichment item to which most students rarely have access.

This situation will not be corrected until there is a clear understanding of how technology can fit easily and naturally into the day-to-day work of our classrooms. There are a few difficult-to-shake misconceptions that must be addressed before we can gain headway.

A prime example stems from the old dichotomy—do we teach about technology, or do we teach with it? In this lamentably widespread confusion, the use of computers is viewed as yet more content to teach, another set of chores to be added to an already-overburdened schedule.

That word processing and desktop publishing provide immeasurable help to professional writers is unquestioned. But harnessing these powerful tools to support youngsters in learning to write is deferred due to the misapprehension that they represent a weighty additional curriculum to be taught. The understanding that marrying learning the tools of word processing and desktop publishing with learning to write makes both easier to achieve has yet to be entertained seriously. *Considerations of "too much, too hard, and too time consuming" have so far won out.* As a result student writers aren't afforded access to tools that professionals in the field consider essential. This book will illustrate how all areas of learning can be energized and brought back into a realm of celebratory discovery and growth through the appropriate use of available technology.

Time and effort are weighty considerations, but education isn't the only "too busy" field out there. We can look to other fields for models of appropriate change. The world of banking and accounting didn't put off the adoption of computers because it was too busy with calculating, analyzing, and recording data in the old traditional ways. It understood that technology offers infinite advantages and did what was necessary to embrace them. The world of education, despite its full plate, must do so too, or students will continue to be deprived of resources that can make learning easier and more effective in many ways.

Education must make today's knowledge power tools a prominent feature of the learning environment. Its very credibility is at stake. School, society's vehicle for preparing the emerging generation for life in a technology-dominated future, represents the last technology-resistant major institution. Although technology rarely figures as an essential classroom resource, it dominates virtually every other venue in which today's young people spend their time. What message does this send to youngsters in regard to the relative value of school in a world full of technology-powered institutions?

The traditional understanding of school, its purpose and dynamics, must change in order to take advantage of the advances that technology offers. Technology profoundly impacts the ways people manage information and work together. Dealing with all these changes is difficult. While the power of technology to positively affect, even supercharge, intellectual work is readily apparent, it does not fit classic categories associated with school improvement items.

Instructional technology is not a curriculum or a program or a philosophy. It is a powerful enhancement to the learning environment, which will become irrelevant without it. This is a type of change that we have little experience with.

Those of us immersed in today's ongoing conversation about the place and value of technology in education confront this in a disheartening, off-track question that is voiced over and over: Is there any proof? Are there any studies that show that technology improves learning? Well, yes, the studies do exist and the vendors of instructional software and the equipment to run it on are happy to provide them. But this query, although well-intentioned, is extremely shortsighted. *Furthermore, it reveals an inability of the educational sector to work in the box and think out of it simultaneously—to provide the traditional as it evolves past it.*

Twenty-first-century technology is not an academic intervention strategy. And while its presence will contribute to an enriched learning experience through which scores can be raised, it would be an essential classroom resource even if that weren't the case. These days, digital technology amounts to crucial, basic equipment in any environment in which intellectual work is done. The need for its ubiquitous presence in our classrooms should not be debated any more than that of the chalk-board, the book, the no. 2 pencil, or any other previously questioned and now transparent technologies. Failure to make this the case is to deepen and reinforce the glaring disconnect between the artificial environment of school, one that continually piques the distrust of a public that senses how out of step it is, and the learning environment of the real world.

What we are offering our young people without the common use of technology for teaching and learning is a poor approximation of the world of contemporary knowledge and thought. Just as smithed metal goods were no longer emblematic of the richness of manufacturing during the machine age and hand-scribed manuscripts became inadequate to support the study of literature during the Guttenberg era, a print-dominant environment today is a terribly skewed and irrelevant one in which to learn. The shift to a digital platform for information and learning has already happened. The only choice left for the educational sector is to acknowledge this and change; the alternative is to continue to function without availing itself of a series of remarkable advances we have made over the past quarter century.

Perhaps no confusion stands more firmly in the way than that having to do with funding. How much technology is actually needed for us to get started in earnest on crafting a truly worthwhile, end-to-end program of technology-supported instruction across the curriculum? This critical question must be placed squarely in the center of the educational radar screen. There is a vague but pervasive notion that until schools can achieve a level of technology saturation in which computers and their accessories become the visually dominant feature in classrooms that little, if anything, can be done to begin the process of taking advantage of technology to support instruction.

This is absolutely not the case. While obtaining more technology for our schools is an issue, it is no longer the defining one. Computers are present in appreciable quantities in our schools and there is much that can be done with them. The large quantity of underused equipment out there is more than disheartening; it is counterproductive. In an era of tight budgets, underutilized resources stand out like sore thumbs and obscure recognition of their potential. Libraries, design firms, research groups, virtually all organizations that draw on a body of knowledge as the stuff of their daily work, rely on the same types and quantities of equipment that get scant use in our classrooms. Reversing this is largely a matter of understanding the need to do so and making it important.

Technology to support teaching and learning no longer represents the wide-eyed visions of futurists. It is not a novelty with which to enrich the real instructional program. We find ourselves in a world in which engaging youngsters in activities that put them into the virtual world of the Web, the planet-wide shared intellectual workspace of those who do the authentic work of thinking, is tantamount to providing them the possibility of relevant learning. It is bitterly ironic that our schools are the last remaining nook in which technology is not a principal support of core activities. Education must correct that or be horribly out of pace with the rest of the world. Until technology is given its proper role in our instructional programs, twenty-first-century students will not be receiving a twenty-first-century education.

A new approach to education, one that comfortably and effectively takes advantage of technology for teaching and learning, is well within our grasp. The challenges to making our move to the redefined educational environment that this approach represents are not economic, logistic, or even difficult. Rather, they are in our own inability to comprehend the direction in which learning and knowing are evolving as digital technologies become more prominent in their use. In a sense, it is difficult to resist this very natural and logical change, foolish to resist developing an intellectual environment that is infinitely easier than the one we currently inhabit. The technology itself is not difficult to learn or use, at least not in the way that the average knowledge worker will use it. There is no need for elaborate organizational efforts. It is simply a matter of clear thinking, visionary understanding, and the will to do what is overwhelmingly right that is needed. This book will lay the groundwork.

CHAPTER 1

Bits, Bytes, and Yeah Buts

The illiterate of the 21st century will not be those who cannot read and write, but those who cannot learn, unlearn, and relearn.

— Alvin Toffler

Why do educators avoid the greatest innovation to learning to come along in over a century? Can an old-dog institution like education learn new tricks from the technology revolution?

It seems unbelievable. On the one hand, humankind has developed a new set of power tools of the mind, digital technologies that aid immeasurably in the tasks of gathering, analyzing, and processing information, and communicating the results of these activities. On the other hand, teachers, the people to whom our society entrusts the development of young minds, the very guardians of the ideal of education, have largely avoided adopting those tools.

For two decades the prospect of bringing computers into our classrooms in order to broaden education's horizons has been examined, debated, avoided, and fought over. Although technology promises to redefine the deepest goals and methods of teaching and learning, it has only been flirted with, not courted seriously. The conversation around technology for education has gone through numerous phases but has never come close to the type of honest, enthusiastic discussion that a phenomenon of such potential merits.

The epicenter of the issue amounts to defining the role and place of technology in the educational experience. We have worked ourselves far past the "what if" days when simply acquiring computers and Internet connections were weighty issues. Those were the easy problems. The acquisition of these items has, in large part, already been accomplished. The maintenance of a base level of access to technology in schools, too, is not much questioned. No one would open a bank without a sufficient level of access to technology to support it, and this logic increasingly applies to schools as well. We must now get to the same level of certainty about how the technology is to be used and that it is an essential resource for teaching and learning.

Much technology is already in place and available to educators. The issue of access is no longer the defining issue. Instead, bringing the technology that is already in schools into play is a more crucial challenge. In order to accomplish that, we must comprehend the deeper issues of how technology can be used and how it changes the nature of the education we set before our young people.

RESISTANCE TO CHANGE

What would prevent serious, committed practitioners of a noble profession from adopting a promising innovation?

For one thing, the institution of school is inherently resistant to change, especially profound change. Although instructional innovations and innovative ideas and philosophies are constantly shopped and dabbled in by the people in our schools, they either lack stickiness or are co-opted by the culture of status quo maintenance that prevails in the world of schooling. Thus, we've seen the comings and goings of whole language, multiple intelligences, and brain-based education, a few recent examples in the seemingly endless parade of new ideas, philosophies, and practices that are embraced, processed, and ultimately passed over by teachers and those who supervise them.

That the fantastic ideas of the moment are quickly shown the door matters little because they all have their successors. And in the long run they will come back after a few decades wrapped up in one new twist or another, ready for a resurgence of interest and another helping of the limelight. Some leave traces of impact on the reality of the classroom, most do not. None, however, ever usher in the revolution that their creators and adoptive enthusiasts promise. In the end, barring a small degree of influence, instruction remains much as it has always been: doled out in bite-size forty-minute periods (or blocks of several such periods), aimed at the superficial *covering* of content that is "pablumized" and made sufficiently general to be fed to thirty-odd pupils from a one-size-fits-all spoon—all ruled by the exigencies of lunch, bus schedules, attendance taking, conduct management, and the other truly important aspects of school life.

Technology is not another of those "let's reinvent school through gut-wrenching change" ideas. It has the potential to deeply impact the institution because it represents a quiet revolution. The hard structures in place need not be toppled with resulting uncertainty and instability. The ways in which technology can revolutionize the experience of learning are soft because beneath them lie the power of the computer, the massively increased capacity to get more done and get it done better.

Even so, the school institution is so set in its ways that the initial confrontation between the teacher and the possibility of change through embracing the unknown has been off-putting. In *The Children's Machine,* author Seymour Papert (1993) describes the frequent early response to the emerging presence of computers in schools as "an immune reaction . . . School acted like any living organism in defending itself against a foreign body" (p. 40).

THE TRAINING FACTOR

After two decades of experience in this area, some definite patterns have emerged. One consideration barring the way that appeared early on has been the perceived need to train teachers to use computers. As the pretechnology era cohort of teachers retires and is replaced with people who use computers comfortably, one would expect that the adoption of the computer as a teaching and learning resource would have become popular. Most disappointingly, for the most part, it has not. Understanding how to operate a computer and seeing its advantages for structuring and delivering instruction are two vastly different things. Even if teachers enter their profession knowing how to use technology, we are still left facing a body of practitioners who don't know how to use them for the core activities of their jobs. It is true, however, that where teachers are hired who know how the technology itself is used, there is, blessedly, at least one layer less of consideration that must be removed for them.

WHERE'S THE CURRICULUM?

To many it may seem improbable that teachers are uncertain and unmotivated in adopting the ultrapowerful tools of technology. What is there about using this set of resources that could possibly appear to be less than inviting to professional educators? To understand this, we must peel away a layer of separation between the public's generalized understanding of the process of education and what actually goes on in the classroom. In truth, teachers in large part have become implementers.

They implement curricula and for the most part don't create it. Curricula, the fuel for what teachers and students do all day, are sometimes generated by universities, sometimes by state and local education departments, and very frequently by commercial providers. Teachers implement mountains of textbooks and related items produced by educational publishers. What they don't do is fully create their own curricula.

Yes, they may create scenarios in which a material, like a trade picture book for instance, is presented to their students and for which they have developed, or more probably adapted, a series of focus questions and a follow-up activity or two. However, it is rare to encounter many teachers nowadays with the creativity, expertise, and confidence to create something from scratch. It is even truer that teachers rarely, if ever, write the content-bearing text that they will put before their students' eyes as the stuff of the day's lesson.

The result is a serious disconnect between teachers' needs for "curriculum" and the availability of sufficient curriculum to support the use of computers. Teachers who may see the value of technology as a powerful support for teaching and learning are often left with the task of creating that curriculum themselves, something that they are most often incapable of or unwilling to do. It is doubly disappointing that while this needed curriculum may exist "out there" somewhere in little pieces that could be cobbled together to assemble a vast mountain of possibilities, teachers don't know where to find it and, alas, those charged with supporting teachers are even less astute about technology, and fail to support them.

There is an odd catch-22 at play here, as well. For the most part, the vast majority of the hundreds of instructional software titles on the market are meant to be ancillary materials. Because schools have traditionally thought of computers as an extra, not as a core, mission-critical resource in the delivering of instruction, software developers have avoided sinking development funds into software that would be considered primary materials for teachers. This has been a self-fulfilling prophecy. Furthermore, teachers are even less likely to try the use of computers as an instructional modality that is used only periodically. Unless a method or practice is something that they can rely on consistently to aid them with their everyday workload, they are not likely to try it.

In the end, with their overwhelming workload exacerbated by scant preparation time, there are few teachers willing to put in the laborious hours every day to research technology resources, align them to the curriculum they are mandated to teach, and account for the very difficult logistics and classroom management issues that come with switching to a new modality.

LACK OF TIME

No "yeah but" has stood in the way of the appropriate educational adoption of technology more than that of time. The time issue cuts to the very core of the problem. It is intrinsically tied to the lack of understanding of how technology can function as a resource that positively impacts teaching and learning across the curriculum. Whatever the variation of the time consideration, underneath it lies the assumption and misapprehension that technology is a separate discipline, a discrete content. To concede that technology may represent an important body of knowledge is useful. But to persist in holding that it is, indeed, a separate subject to be taught in its own time and place is to defeat the very reasons why it was invented in the first place. *It is there to empower the core curriculum areas,* not *to establish a new one.*

The result is an "either/or" mentality in which the practitioner with well-intentioned conscientiousness confesses that with so much to be taught, "Where are we going to get the time to teach technology?" But of course this is a misperception. While technology itself can be offered as a specialized subject, this is not its special value and not the approach that educators should take with it. *In short, the value of computers, Internet, and the like, is as a resource to teach* with, *not as a subject to teach* about. It is a resource that can make the learning of traditional core subject matter, like writing, earth science, and algebra, easier and more effective. Seen this way, considerations that present technology as a subject that threatens to consume valuable instructional time are totally off the mark, In fact, technology can create additional time for instruction.

TECHNOLOGY IS TOO HARD TO LEARN

The other killer "yeah but" that prevents the adoption of technology is the "it's too hard to learn" issue. Yes, what goes on *inside* computers has become mind-bogglingly complex. For technology professionals there is a great deal of difficult-to-acquire knowledge to assimilate. This is a red herring for our discussion, however.

The threshold of knowledge required for teachers and students to get started and gain benefits from using technology are minimal in an era of plug-and-play devices. One takes technology home from the store, unwraps it, plugs it in, and flips the on switch, instantly up and running. Devices now come from the factory with systems and software preinstalled and preconfigured. Beyond that, interactive on-screen wizards and help panels magically appear to explain how to use the machines that run them. The newbie and casual user soon become frustrated with too much on-screen help and follow the simple directions to make them disappear from view.

With today's technology, one simply follows directions to launch and use an application, such as a word processor or a Web browser. The essential skills in operating today's information technology are turn it on, read simple instructions, follow directions, and click the mouse as you are instructed. There is little else needed to get tremendous value from technology. And once started, the skills and understandings build on one another.

Few techno-savvy educators acquired their proficiency through formal training. One of the magical aspects of the technology revolution is that the technology is designed to be intuitive. People learn it by experimenting and then they share what they learned with one another. Think about it this way: what do the R&D guys in Silicon Valley obsess over as they lay awake at night? They dream about ways to get the technology to do more and how to make it easy to use—the key to success in selling it to the public.

UNCLEAR VISION

If teachers could see the situation for what it truly is, they would adopt technology to help them create a better educational experience for their students. But it is not simply teachers who need to be imbued with a fresh and unprejudiced understanding. Those who supervise them do an equal disservice through an unclear vision.

The serious bumps in the road to success for New York City's Project Smart Schools—its massive program to put students and technology together—were largely set in place by a lack of understanding. The project involved a great many people over the years, many of whom bring different perspectives to understanding it in hindsight. Here's one from Norm Scott, a retired NYC educator who spent thirty-five years teaching in the New York City school system in Brooklyn, thirty of them teaching in elementary classrooms and computer labs. He spent his last five as a Project Smart staff developer.

When asked to reflect on why teachers are not embracing technology in any percentage large enough to really make a difference, Scott related,

> In 1996, the NYC government made one of the most interesting attempts ever to impact education. $140M was directed at the city's first comprehensive, centralized infusion of computers and related technology into its classrooms. The result was Project Smart Schools.
>
> The basic model called for four computers and one printer networked to all the computers to be installed in every classroom.

Even with this startling degree of funding, there was only enough money to install computers in a small segment of the school system. Where to begin the school system's new direction in embracing technology-supported instruction was vital. That decision would be a major determinant in Project Smart's success.

Many felt that logically the way to do this was to start at the lower grades and move the program gradually up to higher ones. Technology educators made this point to the implementers, who were primarily administrators and information technologists who had little if any background in implementing programs of this nature. The experts were ignored and Project Smart became a middle school program.

What was wrong with the middle school concept? Teachers, locked in to forty to forty-five minute periods, often with high class sizes, could not figure out a way to make four computers work for them. As one of the Project Smart staff developers I made regular visits to schools. We were most successful when we had projects and group work going. But few, if any, middle school teachers taught that way.

We found it so difficult to make computers an integral part of the program; we relied on short-term projects that could be completed in a finite period of time. Children needed so much support that without the presence of a second adult in the room, projects often bogged down and between visits of the staff developer little progress was made. Teachers were just too busy doing all the things required of them in forty-five minutes with a class to deal with distracting issues related to technology (how do we save our work, where do we save it, why won't it print, how to use the software, etc.).

Teachers did begin to use the computers during their free time, often inviting children to join them. But the major use of the computers by teachers was for their work: lessons, grades, etc., and there was a significant upgrade in their skills as districts began to offer courses in technology. But that upgrade was occurring throughout society and cannot be solely attributed to the program.

When the program was added to elementary schools it had more initial success because most teachers had self-contained classes and more time with the children. But the same tech-related issues kept arising and the staff developers more and more became glorified technicians. For example, after every vacation we had to run all over the district helping teachers restore their networks so they could print.

As pressures on teachers to teach to the tests increased, year by year we had less and less success. With more and more test prep taking up so much classroom time, the technology program was the first to go. Most principals only asked that the computers remain uncovered and left on for show. In some districts there was pressure to make the computers work as part of the test prep program. Expensive computer-assisted software was brought for classrooms and computer labs. In essence, the computers were being turned into electronic workbooks.

The most success was experienced in the early grades where teachers had more options and freedom to teach, but year after year even these grades were being squeezed to do more test prep. Ironically, districts with a so-called more progressive curriculum with a lot of group work that would make computers a more natural component, often had weak tech programs. One of the reasons was that they put all their resources into teacher training, not for technology, but for their pet programs. Sometimes they even "stole" the Project Smart people away.

Another factor was the passing-by of the key tech people in the schools, often the lab teachers who were left out of the process completely. These people had spent years being the only tech source in the schools and their knowledge and insights were totally ignored.

What I would have done?

1. Provide a computer for every teacher to use from his or her desk connected to the Internet. Provide extensive training in the use of this computer. Don't bring in how the children would use the computer until the teacher was totally comfortable.
2. Start in K–2 and put as many computers as needed, six or more, so that the computer becomes part of the fabric of the teaching. In that way children will become proficient enough so that as the program moves up the line they will carry the technology along with them.
3. Do not force-feed this to teachers. Provide a significant number of computers to teachers who feel they are ready to use them.
4. Systems should be designed by people at the school level. Discover key tech people in each school and district/region and create a city-wide culture.
5. Technicians were as necessary as staff developers. Constant breakdowns in software, the difficulty of protecting the computers from damage, and so on, created havoc in some places. (Scott, 2003)

Norm's comments point out, through the benefit of far deeper experience than the actual decision makers had and the luxury of hindsight, the complex dynamics that came into play in the implementation of the project.

The kaleidoscope of implementation factors shifts quickly in the technology issue. Project Smart's big "if" had to do with the risky question, "could" computers be put in classrooms? Now, just a few years down the road, this is no longer a sensible question. We are smack in the midst of grappling with what must we do with those computers and the rest of the technology which will surely show up at the doorsteps of schools continually.

ALL THE TECHNOLOGY WE NEED

Here are a couple of interesting asides to the question, Can we possibly afford to get our hands on technology in any appreciable amounts?

The scarcity edge has been smoothed from the situation. First, technology prices continue to plummet. Even computer prices in retail stores are down to roughly one-quarter to one-third of what they were just three to five years ago. In addition, the business sector has increasingly come to rely on PCs as essential equipment. Every sort of business, from neighborhood pet groomer to manufacturers and retailers of international standing, replace their computers in a continual cycle of purchase, upgrade, discard, and replace. Hundreds of thousands of used but viable computers are discarded each year. This is a vast source of ripe fruit that has not been picked with any regularity by most school systems. Truly, acquiring the equipment for technology-based education is a function of the desire and will to do so and not of the means.

One further observation: those who habitually bemoan the funding consideration in this discussion do so from the outmoded thought habit of either/or—either we buy the technology items we *might* need or we buy the traditional school items that we *know* we need. However, this is not necessarily the case. If a class is going to get its social studies content, for instance, from the Internet, then does the school need to buy social studies textbooks? A thing of beauty that frequently results in little more than putting strain on young backs who have to tote them around all day, social studies texts can cost $80 a piece. A new class set of these texts would set a school back $2,400. That's for just one subject while content across the curriculum is available online free.

The dynamics here are complex and this is not the place for an in-depth discussion about the funding, appropriateness of spending, for example, of our nation's addiction to textbooks. A few thousand dollars that would be used to purchase a set of texts, the very items that may guarantee school irrelevance in the digital age, could certainly be directed at the requirements to truck, install, and network a batch of computers donated from the business sector.

IT'S TOO VALUABLE TO USE

Frequently technology acquisition does not result as part of an organic process in which teachers come to see the potential for technology items and then request them. All too often, we see a "one-shot-deal" effort to bring technology into schools overnight. Often this is done by a principal or school board who, through winning a grant or some other school funding lottery, decides in one fell swoop to shove the twenty-first century down the throats of subordinates. And of course, attendant to this is the hope to never again face the annoying "so where are your computers?" question.

In such school environments teachers often adopt "it's too valuable to risk taking out of the closet" behavior. Teachers who receive technology that they don't request, understand, or want are often intimidated by its presence. They are not used to being entrusted with resources of such great monetary value. Fear of breakage or loss keeps many a computer gathering dust in closets where it is safe from theft, vandalism, and the wear and tear of ordinary usage. But what a tragedy! The shelf life of technology equipment is relatively short—three to five years. Far better to get it into play rather than hoard it away from potential thieves and hungry young minds. But of course, the true culprit again is lack of understanding.

WHERE/HOW TO DEPLOY TECHNOLOGY

If logistically, middle school is not a good choice for the placement of computers, where should they be deployed? A couple of years back there was a good deal of hoopla about the release by the Alliance for

Childhood of a report it commissioned entitled *Fool's Gold: A Critical Look at Computers and Childhood.*

This well-intentioned report inadvertently makes as good a case for the adoption of technology in early childhood settings as it does against it, if one actually probes more than the very surface of the issues that the report purports to explore.

Among the findings reported, "computers pose serious health hazards to children. The risks include repetitive stress injuries, eyestrain, obesity, social isolation, and, for some, long-term physical, emotional, or intellectual developmental damage" (p. 13). A strong statement and one that must be heeded. But what it really reveals is an automatic assumption that the only way that computers can be used with youngsters, and the way that they actually are being used most often, has to do with sitting youngsters for long stretches at a time, one to a terminal, in a computer lab. The authors of the report are probably correct; this is not a good approach to take for younger students. But this is not the only way that technology can be employed to enrich learning.

Why aren't we offered a vision of a teacher bringing the world into the classroom over the Internet? A vision in which the Web delivers to the teacher, not the student, some gem of content unavailable by other means. A vision in which through the use of a large-screen monitor or LCD projector the teacher shares this content with the youngsters. Such a vision presents us with a corollary of how early elementary teachers present books.

It would not be appropriate to teach literature to emergent readers by giving them each a copy of a book and turning them loose to read it on their own. Instead, in the early grades the teacher engages youngsters in a wide variety of prereading activities. In these, the social fabric of the class supports valuable constructivist-oriented discussions. When the book is presented to the youngsters, it is often as a big book, an oversize version of the work that is comprehended and analyzed by the whole group. Later, the students may be directed for short periods to confront their own individual version of the work, supported by one-on-one and small group discussions with the teacher, who mediates and humanizes the experience so that it is developmentally appropriate for the youngsters.

Why, then, when computers enter the school, does all the hard-won wisdom that has gone into developing the rich and nourishing approaches to literacy instruction fly out the window?

The report's executive summary goes on to state, "The emphasis on technology is diverting us from the urgent social and educational needs of low income children" (p. 3). Again it is easy to see that this conclusion is arrived at without consideration of how technology might support, rather than detract from, these needs. Let's look at a previous form of technology, radio, which is still a valuable medium in our society. We know that radios can be purchased with headphones for isolated use or they can be used in social situations. The technology doesn't make this decision, the users do.

For a long time radio strengthened familial bonds in our society. In radio's heyday, listening to the sole radio in a household, the fancy console model that dominated the living room of households during the 1920s, 1930, and 1940s, was the family group's event of the evening. Not only wasn't the presence of the radio isolating, but it drew individuals out of their newspaper and magazine, novel, and crossword puzzle isolation and back into a social relationship.

The report states, "The sheer power of information technologies may actually hamper young children's intellectual growth. Face-to-face conversation with more competent language users, for example is the one constant factor in studies of how children become expert speakers, readers, and writers. Time for real talk with parents and teachers is critical" (p. 3). But the authors are assuming that after the online experience of listening to a speech by Mandela, looking at a mural by Diego Rivera, reading an essay by Saphire or a story by Twain, or listening to music recorded by Kitaro or Sting, they won't be engaged by a competent, caring adult in a discussion of what they have come across and what it really means. The technology doesn't preclude this from happening. If anything, it provides greater grist for the mill of student–teacher interaction. The technology is not driving this car, we are; or we should be!

Again, the report attempts to do a public service by debunking what its preparers took as truisms about computers and their use by youngsters. It asks, "Do computers really motivate children to learn faster and better?" But this is the wrong question. If we want youngsters, as part of their education, to learn how to understand knowledge in the world in which they live, that must include, in very large measure, knowledge that has been prepared for and deposited digitally on the Web. That's where the knowledge is.

A good example of this will take us back to the world of literature written for young readers. Yes, the books of writers like Tomie de Paola, Sandra Cisneros, Gary Soto, or Faith Ringgold still are composed of a few dozen sheets of paper sandwiched between two slices of cardboard and in that sense reading books hasn't changed. But acquiring literacy skills means learning *about* books, too. Not just reading them.

Author studies are part of the curriculum. Want information about the authors of the books that youngsters read? You must go to the Web. That's where the authors themselves have placed information for their young readers, where they give facts about themselves and their motivation for writing, and those delicious insiders' insights and anecdotes about the autobiographical nature of their work. That's where they invite youngsters to correspond with them via e-mail and show youngsters pictures of themselves when they were young. What there is to know about the books and the people who write them is infinitely richer now that the Internet has come along. To deny youngsters this, and to do so when the existence of such technology is one of the most defining aspects of the age in which they are growing up, doesn't make any sense.

The authors of *Fool's Gold* are right about some things. Don't put computers into elementary classroom because the kids will have to know about them to get good jobs twenty years down the road. Yes, "the technology in schools will be obsolete long before five-year-olds graduate." But do put it into their classrooms because it can enrich their learning and offer them increased opportunities for success as learners. And by the way, while those computers may be obsolete, the attitude of embracing innovation and newer technology will stand them in good stead and should be inculcated into their educational experiences.

Computing may not be a make it or break it skill in the future, but speaking clearly and effectively will be. Just when the art of public speaking, something neglected in schools for quite a while, had been given the last rites, a technology came along that resurrected it in the business place. PowerPoint, Microsoft's slide-show format presentation software, made getting up in front of groups and illuminating and convincing them something anyone could do effectively. Some tech-savvy teachers have understood this and through the use of this type of software have given public speaking, one of the five essential skills areas of the language arts subject area, a new life.

Many educators thought they would never see this area of learning come back to life. Not only has the technology made this possible, but it has made it so easily and with an excitement that could not have been anticipated. Yes, as the report states, "strengthening bonds between teachers, students, and families is a powerful remedy for troubled students and struggling schools. Overemphasizing technology can weaken those bonds" (p. 3). So why overemphasize it? Use it, rather, to strengthen the bonds. But above all, don't deprive youngsters of its benefits.

True, "children need live lessons that engage their hands, hearts, bodies, and minds—not computer simulations" (Alliance for Childhood, p. 3). But how much more relevant and powerful those teacher-led live lessons are when the content for them is pulled from the greatest depository of knowledge the human race has ever assembled, the Internet.

FINAL WORD: THE LITANY OF YEAH BUTS

Fool's Gold (and other position items like it) conveys the scope of misunderstanding about how technology is being used in schools, how it can be used, and what it offers us as we provide educational experiences for ourselves and our fellow humans. Perhaps we foolishly bought into the idea that the technology, because it is so powerful, would do it all for us. Or perhaps those who enjoy sounding the alarm have been overzealous. Technology won't handle the work of education for us. Education is a natural function, a form of human growth. It is part of the process of life and it requires constant effort on our parts as well as nourishment, something that technology will provide.

The litany of "yeah buts" about adopting technology to support teaching and learning is long. As these considerations are brought to the light of day for close examination, however, it is easy to see that they merit little standing as solid arguments. All of them have been surmounted somewhere close to home. We can discover how to get past the "yeah buts." Technology is not too costly nor too hard to learn how to use, nor is it terribly difficult to understand how it can enhance education. It will not rob us of valuable time; rather, it can free time up for important things. It will not harm youngsters nor force inappropriate materials or experiences on them. We would do well to take full advantage of it in the field of education. It is not something we can avoid.

CHAPTER 2

What's at Stake?

We have, in effect, been committing an act of unthinking, unilateral educational disarmament.

—National Commission on Excellence in Education, *A Nation at Risk: The Imperative for Educational Reform* (1983)

> How does technology transform teaching and learning? Where is this transformation happening and what does it look like?

The message is extraordinary and irrefutable: The longer our children are exposed to our public school system the farther they fall behind. Even our very best math students can't compete with their counterparts around the world. Our top kids are last among 16 countries that test physics and math achievement.

All of this or some version of it has been the condition of public education for as long as I've been involved in this struggle. And that's about 30 years. But even after three largely frustrating decades, at no time have I felt a greater sense of urgency about this fight or the stakes we're playing for.

The above statement is from a speech by Lou Gerstner, then CEO of IBM. It was delivered at the 1999 National Education Summit, an event held periodically at which national leaders, including presidents, governors, and education, business, and civic leaders of every stripe, convene to discuss the state of education.

The sentiment in Gerstner's speech is similar to that expressed at previous and subsequent summits. It is quite likely the predominant feeling the general public has about public schools as well.

WHAT'S AT STAKE?

When we consider the adoption of technology to support education, what's at stake? The whole ball of wax, that's what's at stake! Contemporary education, at least as it is played out in its primary delivery vehicle, the institution we call school, is foundering. School gets a no-confidence vote from students, parents, and concerned citizens alike. While it is impossible to get professionals and laypeople to agree on precisely what we are trying to accomplish in education, what its goals and measures of success should be, there seems to be a great deal of agreement that school is failing.

Professional educators address this by attempting endless refinements to the system we have in place: better instructional practices and methods, improved curricula and approaches to developing and disseminating them, and on and on. Could it be that they haven't framed the challenge properly? Could it be that school has become largely irrelevant?

This assertion is not far-fetched if examined objectively. A walk through a typical classroom today will not reveal much that departs radically from classrooms of fifty or even a hundred years ago. And this, in a world in which change is the only constant of consequence. After touring the classroom, take a walk to a local store where digital video games and media products are sold. Never mind the space hunt, shoot-'em-up content of many of the games; observe, rather, the remarkable way today's youngsters interface with them, as they do with websites, DVDs, MP3 players, or any of the technology-supported consumer products that flood their world. All of them present their content in a manner that is experienced as intensely and satisfyingly personal to youngsters.

They are interactive in ways that young consumers find compelling. In the aggregate, they establish an intellectual play space that was created in response to the needs and desires of the emerging citizenry of the new millennium. It is an intellectual environment in which media items present themselves to young consumers simultaneously as totally individualized experiences *and* as pathways into a community of individuals sharing the same experiences, interests, and worldview. It is a realm in which hungry young minds are free to roam about hyperlinking and making important connections. A space in which they may engage in the free-form intellectual feeding frenzies needed to satisfy their mental growth spurts.

The fact that today's youth have sampled and have become passionate residents of choice of this digital intellectual play space represents a double challenge for school. Not only is it the alternative learning platform of choice, but it powerfully overshadows the traditional space of school.

The good news is that school can incorporate the same technology into much of what it does and transform itself in the process. It is laudable that our professional educators continue to struggle with new curriculum program after new program as they try to force ever more mileage out of a vehicle that is worn out and exhausted. But perhaps it is not a matter of climbing Mount Everests of cognitive theory and pedagogy. What if there were something simpler and easier to be done? Our youngsters are not learning as we wish they would largely because we have not done what it takes to engage them and have not provided the tools needed to succeed once engaged. It is all about engagement! Why not adopt a set of new resources that will guarantee that engagement?

The ways that the digital intellectual play space can be used as a platform to deliver content to students are endless. Let's examine a sampling of the ways that technology can revolutionize teaching and learning. Actually, it already has revolutionized it, but in the absence of a critical mass of users, the result is hard to perceive against the overwhelming background static of traditional instructional activities that drown it out.

Reading

There are many ways in which reading can be facilitated or enhanced by the use of technology as a resource. There is software, much of it

available for free on websites, that illustrates the mechanisms and concepts of phonemes and phonics. There are "electronic flash card"
pieces that drill on basics, allowing teachers to save their face-to-face
time for instruction of a more challenging nature. And there are utilities, like online dictionaries and thesauri, lists of vocabulary words, and
similar items. But more importantly, there are aspects of the study of
reading that truly are transformed by technology.

Author and genre studies are good examples. Want to learn about an
author you've been assigned to read or whose work you've grown to
appreciate? Look for websites put up by the author or publisher. There
you'll find out all the juicy stuff about who this person is, why he
writes what he does, his feelings and advice about writing, what he
likes to read personally, the name of his dog, and on and on. Looking
for more titles by the same author, or books written in the same vein?
Want to read summaries of books in a given genre to supplement your
understanding of it as you read some complete works? Care to peruse
reviews of books by other students, professional reviewers, or the authors themselves? Accomplishing these things before the Internet
would have represented a series of very labor-intensive chores. Now
doing so is easy and exciting.

Software engines, such as the proprietary engine used by Achieve3000
(www.achieve3000.com), will take any text and prepare the reading material to meet the reading level of each student. Finding relevant and appropriate material that is suitable for youngsters is often difficult, the
reading level issue makes it immeasurably more so. Achieve3000 makes
it much easier to ensure that an otherwise perfect piece of literature is
useful for the specific needs of youngsters.

Writing

Of the tens of thousands of professional writers in the world, few
write without the aid of a word processor. And even those few are ed-
ited and published by others who use computers. If this technology has
become the standard for professionals, shouldn't youngsters be afforded the same tools as they learn to write, a vital life skill?

It isn't simply that the word processor spits out a legible final copy,
something that is a boon to student writers, but the entire process of

writing, from prewriting outlining to early drafts through revision and final copy, is facilitated greatly by technology. Don't worry about spell and grammar checkers. Many professionals will tell you that the constant, gentle but unrelenting, nonjudgmental corrections in these areas that they have gotten as their skill has matured have actually allowed them to improve their spelling and grammar.

Math

Calculating was the original application of computers, but the computer's value goes far beyond its calculator function in facilitating the learning of numbers. Many of today's top math educators talk about "numeracy" being a primary goal, developing students' number sense. The computer allows youngsters to visualize numbers and how they behave. Want to understand the meaning of a fraction? You can express it traditionally, but with software the fraction can be converted into a line, bar, or pie graph instantly, changed at will in a fluid dance of numbers that wasn't possible before.

Science

With the new digital technology we can promote science learning as never before. Science is an area of teaching in which familiarity with the content of the subject is crucial. Unfortunately, over the past several decades, there has been an extreme shortage of teachers who know science content. The vast science resources available on the Web, like those on the NASA website and the TryScience website, can help any generally educated person prepare himself to teach science.

More importantly, the technology can engage youngsters through types of experiences that previously were unavailable. One dimension of this has to do with visualization and interactivity, aspects of learning that are easily achieved through the use of online software. An example of this is the Hubble space telescope website. Students can view a dynamically changing illustration that shows over which part of our planet the telescope can be found at any given moment.

Scientists have placed robotic digital probes around the world to gather data for a variety of purposes. Much of this data is free on websites and can be used with students in real-time data-based projects. To bring alive the effect of earth's rotation on local heat, wind speed, and so on, the teacher can direct youngsters to weather data collected by technology and reported on websites.

Simulations are a unique way that technology can illustrate concepts and engage students. Online buoyancy simulation software is a common example. As the student chooses variables, such as the weight of an object and the type of liquid medium it is in, the software automatically illustrates its position in the medium through an engaging animation that changes and gives a unique experience to each student who uses it.

Want a complete guide to creating a science museum in your classroom? It's on the Smithsonian Museum website.

The world's smaller creatures are thankful for technology now that the dissection of frogs and a host of other animals ordinarily cut up in biology classes can be handled virtually through software found free on the Web.

Social Studies

Technology offers a totally reinvigorated experience in history, geography, economics, and political science, the four areas of social studies. It also offers opportunities to cross-pollinate them in mixed projects as well. Here are just a few examples:

Across the top of the website www.ourdocuments.gov is a moving parade of icons arranged chronologically. Each of these is one of 100 essential documents in the history of the United States. Click on one of them and a dynamic photo of the actual document appears. This can be saved and printed out for closer study. Accompanying this is text explaining the history and significance of the document. How else would a student get his hands on a copy of the original papers for *Brown v. Board of Education,* congressional censure of Senator McCarthy, or *Plessy v. Ferguson*? This can be done now in a two-minute visit to the site and without interruption of the flow of study from the youngster's bedroom or classroom.

Go to Kidsbank.com for animated lessons on interest rates, electronic funds transfer, and how checks work. Youngsters can compete in making virtual investments by playing The Stock Market game online, too.

Where is Vanuatu? Go to the National Geographic Xpeditions site (www.nationalgeographic.com/xpeditions) and use its map database engine to find the answer. Or create a climate map of a region of the world and e-mail it to a friend on this site.

What do you think, should land in developing nations be controlled by local people or by the government in the capital? Read, consider, reflect, vote, and then debate with youngsters from around the world on this issue at the website of software producer Tom Snyder Productions (www.teachtsp2.com/cdonline). It's free.

Arts

Log on to http://daphne.palomar.edu/design, where students can join design teacher Jim Saw at Palomar College, view the examples he has posted, and e-mail him questions or opinions.

Or perhaps you'd like to learn how to create pointillist art in the style of Seurat. Go to the Crayola website (www.crayola.com) for that.

What do Fats Waller, Bessie Smith, and Langston Hughes have in common? Go to the Kennedy Center's Drop Me Off in Harlem website (www.artsedge.kennedy-center.org/exploring/harlem) and find out about this neighborhood's rich history in which they and many other kindred spirits soared.

Want the world to appreciate a youngster's drawing? Submit it to Artsonia (www.artsonia.com) or the many other sites that post a scanned file of it online in a virtual gallery.

BY USING TECHNOLOGY TO LEARN, YOUNGSTERS LEARN ABOUT TECHNOLOGY

The way for our young people to learn about technology concepts and skills is to use them within the context of their overall education. While a small percentage of the upcoming generation may be on a track to directly enter the technology industry, most of today's students are not.

Students are coming of age in a society in which all workers, citizens, and consumers will use technology constantly. But they won't, for the most part, receive formal training in its use. If that were needed, the technology simply wouldn't be adopted. It would be too impractical.

Two good examples of this are the ATM and the automated supermarket checkout. Beyond the initial getting acquainted first trial use or two, there is little to learn and little to know about using these ubiquitous computing devices. This is the model of technology use that continues to make technology essential, as opposed to the type of deep learning curve associated with setting up a database for a bank or a network for an HMO.

What youngsters need to know about technology has more to do with understanding how it satisfies human needs, how it changes the flow of learning, knowing, and communicating, than it does with electronics and programming. They need to know this from the point of view of the learner. This means understanding how things were done before the technology arrived and making meaningful comparisons. It also means understanding it from the point of an active, informed consumer. This perspective is the impetus for new technology developments, a crucial aspect of citizen participation in a technology-supported environment.

Again, the best way, perhaps the only way, to bring students to these crucial understandings is to have them use technology actively in the context of their work as learners, and then to provide them adequate opportunities and places to reflect on their experience. That is technology education for the twenty-first century. And no amount of instruction in the mere mechanics of technology will provide it. We are not talking about the mere reveling in gizmos, but the study of humankind's solutions to problems. Among a great many other windows that technology opens is a remarkable entrance to the realm of meta-cognition, thinking about thinking and learning about learning.

Advances and innovations in digital technology—computers, Internet, e-mail, and so on—have to be understood within the context of the phenomenon of technology in the broader, older sense of the word. This has been largely ignored. In New York State, for instance, there has been a requirement for a course in technology for eighth graders for a good number of years. School systems within the state have, for the most part, failed to satisfy that requirement. Understandably, if nontechnology-savvy school administrators mistakenly assume that they must choose between providing instruction in basic literacy or math *or* in technology they will skimp on technology as a "frill" every time. Sadly, this common scenario provides a good example of well-intentioned individuals depriving youngsters of an opportunity to learn one of the things most necessary to function in the twenty-first century. It is done as part of a desperate attempt to get caught up on delivering an education that was designed for the nineteenth century.

The reflective understanding of technology, the contextualized use of technology to support core subjects, can provide a relevance and motivation that beating the dead horse of traditional methods at the exclusion of the new cannot!

One essential aspect of life in the digital age that youngsters must learn is content and presentation sophistication. Because the technology has changed our level of access to information from one of scarcity to that of surfeit, the mere publishing of ideas can no longer be considered tantamount to legitimizing them. Today's citizen of the global intellectual environment must be able to evaluate the source, motivation of production, and the quality of what is published and above all its suitability to the purpose at hand.

In his well-known article "Teaching Zack to Think," writer Alan November (1998) relates how a student found an article on the Internet that purported to prove that the Holocaust never happened. In this anecdote, the teacher has to introduce the youngster to the sophistication skills needed to understand that content is published for many reasons other than purely objective, responsible reporting. In the digital age, when self-publishing is easy and difficult to distinguish from more sanctioned forms, one must be very vigilant when confronting it. This article was written roughly a decade ago. Since then, the amount of content, especially objectionable content, has burgeoned. Spam has exploded, and even prosaic forms of content must be dealt with employing a new set of intellectual skills developed for living in the maturing information age.

A COMPLETELY DIFFERENT SORT OF CURRICULUM

ISTE (International Society for Technology in Education) has worked on defining what students should know and should be able to do with technology. But these understandings and competencies do not compose a curriculum in the usual sense of the word.

On the one hand, they do make up a body of knowledge, a list of things to know. This amounts to content, the principle element of any curriculum. But on the other hand, in the aggregate, they constitute a new *context* for how to learn and process knowledge, a completely different sort of curriculum.

The ISTE website (http://cnets.iste.org/students/s_stands.html) lists the student technology understandings and competencies as follows:

Technology Foundation Standards for Students
1. Basic operations and concepts
    • Students demonstrate a sound understanding of the nature and operation of technology systems.
    • Students are proficient in the use of technology.
2. Social, ethical, and human issues
    • Students understand the ethical, cultural, and societal issues related to technology.
    • Students practice responsible use of technology systems, information, and software.
    • Students develop positive attitudes toward technology uses that support lifelong learning, collaboration, personal pursuits, and productivity.
3. Technology productivity tools
    • Students use technology tools to enhance learning, increase productivity, and promote creativity.
    • Students use productivity tools to collaborate in constructing technology-enhanced models, prepare publications, and produce other creative works.
    • Students use productivity tools to collaborate in constructing technology-enhanced models, prepare publications, and produce other creative works.
4. Technology communications tools
    • Students use telecommunications to collaborate, publish, and interact with peers, experts, and other audiences.
    • Students use a variety of media and formats to communicate information and ideas effectively to multiple audiences.
5. Technology research tools
    • Students use technology to locate, evaluate, and collect information from a variety of sources.
    • Students use technology tools to process data and report results.

- Students evaluate and select new information resources and technological innovations based on the appropriateness for specific tasks.
6. Technology problem-solving and decision-making tools
   - Students use technology resources for solving problems and making informed decisions.
   - Students employ technology in the development of strategies for solving problems in the real world.

IN SHORT, TODAY'S YOUNGSTERS NEED SOMETHING THEY ARE NOT CURRENTLY GETTING

In their article entitled "Educating Billy Wang for the World of Tomorrow," authors Marcelo Suarez-Orozco and Howard Gardner (2003) state, "How should we envision an education for the new millennium? More than any generation before them, today's children need to develop the cognitive skills that allow them to work comfortably with new and evolving technologies. They need to be able to sift through unprecedented amounts of information to figure out what is true, what is trivial, what is worth retaining, and how to synthesize disparate bits into a meaningful whole" (p. 34).

Suarez-Orozco and Gardner, both professors of stature at Harvard University's graduate school of education, tell the true story of "Billy Wang, student extraordinaire for the new millennium." Billy, an immigrant youth, arrives in the United States with the qualities our schools most value in youngsters: he's bright, disciplined, conscientious, and motivated. He soon distinguishes himself as a high-achieving student. As he moves into his junior year in high school, though, he decides that the world presented to him by his computer is far more interesting and worthwhile than that presented by his school. Although he doesn't drop out, he finds school irrelevant and gets a good deal of his real education in spite of what is offered to him there, not because of it. Billy finds the world exciting but school "boring."

The authors lament, "The failure to harness Billy's contagious energy is the failure of an education system more in tune with the realities of early-twentieth-century America than with the demands of the twenty-first global century" (p. 34). They see the pandemic failure to

engage young minds to be a failure so profound as to be beyond the re-
demptive reach of high test scores, something that current educational
policymakers point to as irrefutable validation of the present direction
of schooling.

Suarez-Orozco and Gardner point out, however, that "Billy is way
ahead of those policymakers because he understands the character of a
globalized millennium in which we live" (p. 34). Billy understands, they
point out, that "new information and communications technologies connect humans as never before and make available the sum of the world's
information (though not wisdom) at the click of a mouse" (p. 44). They
are talking about the extraordinary effect the new technologies have on
today's young people. Not simply the effect of the machines themselves,
but more importantly, the way they change the very nature of learning,
thinking, and communicating.

Suarez-Orozco and Gardner paint a complex picture of the need for
schools to keep basic literacy and math skills, understandings of historical, scientific, mathematical, and artistic ways of thinking, with, of
course, the addition now of computers and technology. But it is more
than keeping some of the old and adding some of the new to it. There
are brand-new skills that must accompany all of this on several levels.
Students must see the interconnectedness of knowledge in the new millennium. They must learn and understand in a multidisciplinary context. And they need to experience the new ways of the social dynamics
of learning, knowing, and living globally. In short, today's youngsters
need something they are not currently getting.

Twenty-First-Century Skills

Invention is the mother of necessities.

—Marshall McLuhan

When a layer or two is peeled away in the educational technology
discussion, one comes to the core issue of what value is actually represented by the technology. In the beginning, this was attributed to students' need to know about the new digital technologies and how to use
them. Further along, the conversation shifted to the benefits that the
technology affords in fostering, facilitating, and improving teaching

and learning in the traditional subject areas such as literacy, mathematics, science, and social studies. Both of these concepts continue to be valid. However, a third, and perhaps more important, concept has emerged.

The new technologies have been developed to solve needs that have arisen relatively recently in the human experience. The technology has shaped the way people think, learn, and communicate. They do these things differently in the digital information age than they did before. As a result a body of skills has developed that has come to be called twenty-first-century literacy skills.

Schools and other facets of the educational sector must begin to educate with the acquisition of these skills as a high-priority need. Not to be aware of this need and not to address it is tantamount to relegating educational efforts and resources to the context of a previous age. The cost of this is and will continue to be increasingly to render them irrelevant. It is also true that our current digital information age is as intolerant of irrelevance as any age before it and more so than most. We must not allow this to continue.

The Partnership for Twenty-First Century Skills, a consortium of governmental agencies (including the U.S. Department of Education), for-profit technology sector corporations (including Apple, Dell, and Microsoft, among others), and nonprofits (including NEA and ISTE) have done extensive work in analyzing this situation, developing a vision and framework of understanding about it, and have reported on their findings. Their work is aimed primarily at influencing the nature of the educational experience our schools offer young people. Consequently, theirs is a call for dramatic change in schooling.

The consortium takes a position that is calculated to maintain the role and position of school in our society by returning the platform on which it does its business to one of relevance. This is accomplished through a vision that calls for our classically organized schools to continue with traditional instruction in basic skills, but that also has them embrace and include twenty-first-century literacy skills. They state that "both are essential and, when done concurrently, each reinforces the other."

The partnership is made up of disparate bedfellows whose agendas may not mesh as well when they meet in other contexts. Interestingly, the partnership's vision is a comforting one for the educational establishment. It does not call for any apple carts to be upset seriously. Many thoughtful leaders, though, have come to a contrary conclusion about the nature of the change that the report calls for. They feel that new technologies establish a completely new context for knowing and learning, one that takes us far beyond the simplistic context of school.

This context may not be able to coexist peacefully with our contemporary education system, an institution that still clings, in large part, to fact-based learning and employs high-stakes testing to measure quantities of knowledge learned as the standard of success. The new context primarily points to the ongoing acquisition of learning skills as the goal of education, a new idea that is radically different. These two grounds of being may be far more incompatible that one would infer from the tone of the partnership's language.

School is an institution that changes, but with great resistance. To fully redo it to reflect the existence and importance of twenty-first-century skills will require very profound change. Not a change simply in the organizational aspects of school, but to reflect a new understanding of the nature of the very core of school's business. This challenge will likely be felt as a threat. The history of the struggle to infuse technology in our schools shows that many members of this institution find greater comfort in resisting change from the familiar, even if it is to a needed and more sensible future.

What we are really talking about is getting twenty-first-century educators to let go of nineteenth-century practices. Seen from the perspective of twenty-first-century skills, much of the acquisition and superficial use of computers in our schools has actually worked against the permanent, appropriate adoption of technology. Too much activity has been about the mere presence of technology. Consequently, there is little comprehension about the true purpose of its presence in and promise for schools in the first place. This is actually counterproductive to getting on the right track. When a man buys a tool simply because his neighbor has one, he soon becomes disenchanted with its value and presence in his home. He is less likely to use it properly at that point than if he had not acquired it in the first place. Twenty-first-century skills must be comprehended and valued before technology can mean much for our schools.

"Today's education system faces irrelevance unless we bridge the gap between how students live and how they learn. . . . Students will spend their adult lives in a multitasking, multifaceted, technology-driven, diverse, vibrant world—and they must arrive equipped to do so" (*Learning for the 21st Century: A Report and Mile Guide for 21st Century Skills*).

Among the findings and recommendations the report makes are the following:

- *Emphasize Learning Skills.* As much as students need knowledge in core subjects, they also need to know how to keep learning continually throughout their lives. Learning skills comprise three broad categories of skills:
  1. information and communication skills,
  2. thinking and problem-solving skills, and
  3. interpersonal and self-directional skills.
- *Use Twenty-First-Century Tools to Develop Learning Skills.* In a digital world, students need to learn to use the tools that are essential to everyday life and workplace productivity. Skilled twenty-first-century citizens should be proficient in ICT (information and communication technologies) literacy, defined by the Programme for International Student Assessment (PISA) as "the interest, attitude and ability of individuals to appropriately use digital technology and communication tools to access, manage, integrate and evaluate information, construct new knowledge, and communicate with others in order to participate effectively in society."
- *Teach and Learn in a Twenty-First-Century Context.* Students need to learn academic content through real-world examples, application, and experiences both inside and outside of school. Students understand and retain more when their learning is relevant, engaging, and meaningful to their lives. In the global, networked environment of the twenty-first century, student learning also can expand beyond the four classroom walls. Schools must reach out to their communities, employers, community members, and of course, parents to reduce the boundaries that divide schools from the real world.
- *Teach and Learn Twenty-First-Century Content.* Education and business leaders identified three significant emerging content areas that are critical to success in communities and workplaces:
  1. global awareness;
  2. financial, economic, and business literacy; and
  3. civic literacy.

Much of this content is not captured in existing curricula or taught consistently with any depth in schools today. An effective way to incorporate this content is to infuse knowledge and skills from these areas into the curriculum.

There remains, however, a profound gap between the knowledge and skills most students learn in school and the knowledge and skills they need in typical twenty-first-century communities and workplaces.

IT'S IN THE DIGITAL PUDDING

The type of education called for in the report is within our grasp. The greatest challenges to having it for our young people are perceiving the need and exercising the will to satisfy it. The tools to accomplish this are already there, in abundance.

Where's the proof of this? Are there teachers and students currently using technology to facilitate, enrich, and expand the dimensions of learning? Are there examples out there of interesting, inspiring, appropriate technology use? What does one have to do to find examples, particularly those unfettered by the interests of those groups with special agendas regarding technology and education?

We undertook a simple experiment to answer the above questions. Performing Web searches based on simple inquiries like "examples of student technology use" and "classroom technology projects," we attempted to determine how many noteworthy examples of transformative educational technology use could be found and reviewed within fifteen minutes. Not surprisingly, the search engine spat out far more than can be reported in this book. Below is a small part of the random sampling that the search turned up. Readers are encouraged to conduct a similar experiment.

Multicultural Heroes Project
www.ed.gov/pubs/EdReformStudies/EdTech/multicultural.html

Materials produced by the Multicultural Heroes project is archived on the project's website and is available for reference and dissemination to peers and others around the world. There is material here to support teachers in replicating and expanding on this ambitious and relevant work and for youngsters to use directly their own research and development of style and voice as thinkers and communicators.

A multidisciplinary, technology-supported effort in which bilingual fifth grade students at Frank Paul Elementary School in Salinas, California, developed and produced a set of materials (videotapes and written texts), Multicultural Heroes focused on minority leaders, "multicultural heroes," both locally and at the state and national level.

The project brought various areas of the curriculum together: social studies (researching past and present minority leaders, studying the impact of discrimination and learning how individuals dealt with its effects), writing (writing and editing interviews, letters, and narrative texts with a clear sense of purpose and a strong eye toward audience), reading (critical reading of previous literature on minority leaders), arts (graphic design aspects of desktop publishing), oral language skills (developing interview skills), and math (budgeting and managing the cost of producing, marketing, and distributing the tapes).

From a New Teacher to the World
bama.ua.edu/~cook057

Can Ms. or Mr. Average Teacher use technology to make his/her efforts easier to be understood and taken advantage of by students, parents, supervisors, and the world? A recent education graduate from the University of Alabama and a new teacher, offers the world her website as an example. In all probability you will never meet this conscientious young lady, but a simple mouse click will take you to her site. There you will get an instant snapshot of her teaching philosophy, be offered resources that she has culled from throughout the world of math education, get access to her lesson plans for possible collegial interaction or replication, and even be taken into her classroom for a look-see.

Electronic Postcards from around the World
www.genevaschools.org/austinbg/class/gray/internet/electronic

On the server of an Austinburg, Ohio, elementary school is the website of Mrs. Gray's class. The class uses its website to share learning adventures it's had with its project Electronic Postcards from around the World. The site shows some of the many messages the class has received from schools as far off as Australia and China. "To view the Electronic Postcards we have received, click on the map or the list below the map." It also offers other teachers and students everything they'll need to know and have in order to participate in the project themselves. Teacher and class state, "This project offers a fun and exciting way to learn geography and map skills plus provide an increased social awareness of schools/communities around the world. The children will develop and enhance their communication skills by exchanging Electronic Postcards with schools from around the world."

CyberFair
www.globalschoolhouse.org/GSH/cf

Over this project's nine-year history classes from around the world have used a wide variety of technology to carry out and document learning projects. These are class-created projects that use Web authoring as a new medium for expression and communication. They are Web published for the whole world to appreciate and learn from. A couple of examples of the many hundreds of projects archived are an in-depth study of the traditional Chinese lion dance submitted by the Da-Tsuen Elementary School of Chunchua, Taiwan, a portfolio of photos of natural and man-made attractions to be found in Antique Province, Philippines, that was submitted by the Antique National School, and Recipe for a Great Community, an expression of civic pride by students at the Riverdale School in Riverdale, New Jersey. CyberFair, by the way, is but one component of Global Schoolnet, a compendium of numerous such efforts.

enGauge Resources: Success Stories
www.ncrel.org/engauge/resource/stories/index.html

This North Central Regional Laboratory resource features multiple examples of K–12 classrooms that use technology to help students gain twenty-first-century skills. Each example provides background and contact information regarding the example. Some examples include videos of the classroom. Look at the example from Sunnyside Elementary for ways to integrate technology into a primary language arts curriculum.

Is There Life on Mars?
www.cesa10.k12.wi.us/clustera/multimedia/ elevastrum/berge/tech_projects.htm

Is there life on Mars? Check out Kenny's PowerPoint discussion to inform yourself, or any of his classmates' compelling offerings on science and the humanities, for that matter. Elva-Strum Middle School in Wisconsin.

Hurricanes
www.iss.k12.nc.us/schools/scotts/stproj.htm

Everything you need to know about hurricanes is on this website. The fifth graders at Scotts Elementary School, North Carolina, learned about them so that they could teach us.

Students Take Charge of Identifying Teaching Resources
www.westirondequoit.org/technology/technology_project.htm

Interested in teaching youngsters about the Holocaust? It's something that a great many educators will turn their attention to. The students at West Irondequoit High School in New York State have done a good deal of the research and organization for you. Their work is well presented on their website, as well. "This website was designed to help educators, librarians, and parents who are searching for children's literature about the Holocaust. There are many books for children about the Holocaust, some more appropriate than others. Our class has read and reviewed seventeen of them and our reviews reflect our evaluations of the material presented in each one. We hope that the reviews, illustrations, and recordings that we have included on this site will guide you in selecting literature for children on this very complex subject."

World War II Movie
www.lakelandschools.org/lhs/studentshowcase.htm

Among other handsome examples of project embedded technology use posted on the Lakeland High School (Shrub Oak, NY) website is the *World War II Movie*. This flash movie was created as an extra credit project in Mr. Peters's U.S. history and government class. Impressive message, insight, and technical sophistication.

Virtual Quilt
www.ibiblio.org/ephesus/quilt.html

A project like Virtual Quilt could only come about in the age of ubiquitous technology. The project's site explains, "Welcome to the Virtual Quilt Page. Now spanning five continents! The Virtual Quilt is a patchwork panorama of communities from across the world. The idea is that students will create a 'patch' along with a description of how the patch represents their community. Then they submit the patch to the 'seamstresses' at Ephesus Road Elementary School in Chapel Hill, North Carolina and the patch and description are added to the existing quilt." The project is art, literature, play, study, and more.

Invite a Teacher to Sponsor You
www.ncsu.edu/midlink/call.htm

The mission of *MidLink* magazine, a nonprofit organization, is "to highlight exemplary work from the most creative classrooms around the globe. MidLink is the virtual space where any student aged eight to eighteen can be a published author. We prefer classroom projects, sponsored by a teacher, but you can always invite a teacher to sponsor you."

77 Ways
www.isd77.k12.mn.us/resources/techuse.html

Mankato, Minnesota's School District 77 has posted a Web page outlining seventy-seven ways that its teachers use technology as part of their work with youngsters.

Please Click on Our Names to Look at Our Work
www.wccusd.k12.ca.us/washington/web01/projects

Over 2,000 intelligent souls have visited the website of the Washington Elementary School in Port Richmond, California. Join them to view the dozen class projects they have posted there. Recommended is Ms. Curley's fourth grade class Donner Party Project. The project is presented by the class as a collaborative, interactive exhibit of their research into a significant and tragic event in the history of the West, annotated in their own words, and profusely illustrated with their own artwork.

Projects, Projects, Projects, and More Projects
http://k12science.ati.stevens-tech.edu/currichome.html

The website of the Stevens Institute of Technology Center for Improved Science and Engineering (CIESE) displays several portfolios of technology-rich projects representing the participation of over 300 schools. The four categories are collaborative projects, projects using primary sources and archived collections, real-time data projects, and partner projects. Here are some examples:

Collaborative projects. Down the Drain is an Internet-based collaborative project that has students sharing information about water usage with other students from around the country and the world. Based on data collected by their household members and their classmates, students determine the average amount of water used by one person in a day and compare this to the average amount of water used per person per day in other parts of the world.

Projects using primary sources and archived collections. Historical Treasure Chests is a project that has students review primary sources such as letters, diaries, photographs, maps, and artifacts provide authentic materials from the past. Students draw conclusions about the items and formulate their own hypotheses about the time period(s) during which they were created. They are guided to do further research, using secondary sources, that either confirm or challenge their ideas.

Real-time data projects. The Gulf Stream Voyage is an online multi-disciplinary project that utilizes both real-time data and primary source materials to help students discover the science and history of the Gulf Stream. Students investigate the driving forces behind this great ocean current, how it affects the Atlantic Ocean, and some of humankind's experiences dealing with it.

Partner projects. Tropical Biology in Costa Rica is a project in which students interact with materials produced by a professor of biology and a group of college students who embarked on an educational journey deep in the tropical rainforests of Costa Rica and submitted daily logs, photos, and scientific notes investigating the local climate and habitat.

Learning from Harry Truman's Footlocker
www.trumanlibrary.org/whistlestop/teacher_lessons/
integrating_tech.htm

The website of the Truman Presidential Museum and Library. The site displays numerous projects that have been completed by classes participating with the organization and that can be referred to by others in their own work or replicated. One of the many examples available on the site is Exploring Truman's Footlocker: Fifth Grade Class Project.

A presentation based on elementary school students' exploration and research concerning historical items in Harry Truman's footlocker.

FINAL WORD: WITHIN OUR GRASP

All of the products that compose this tip-of-the-iceberg set of examples were produced by ordinary students and teachers in typical schools. That the authors found them is testimony to the fact that technology really does elevate the business of learning from the doing of anonymous futile chores of little import, to that of engagement in exciting authentic activities and having a voice that is heard. The question is, If these youngsters have been given the opportunity to flourish educationally with technology, why can't all of our young people do so?

A moment is at hand in which a crucial, invaluable change for the better can be made. Education, an institution that has been foundering, can be made relevant, vital, and exciting once again through the sensible adoption of technology for use by our young people as they learn and grow. The resources with which this moment can be seized are not beyond our grasp and the benefits of applying them to tasks at hand can easily be comprehended and appreciated if one chooses to. Yes, the institution of school will continue whether or not we are astute enough to take advantage of the extraordinary opportunity the technology revolution represents for it. Its relationship, however, to true education, a natural life process in which people satisfy an irresistible need of their intellectual self, is what will suffer. What's at stake? Everything!

CHAPTER 3

Conceptions, Misconceptions, and Reconceptions: Instructional Technology Misunderstood

Only puny secrets need protection. Big discoveries are protected by public incredulity.

— Marshall McLuhan

Life is a succession of lessons, which must be lived to be understood.

— Ralph Waldo Emerson

How does technology transform teaching and learning? Where is this transformation happening and what does it look like?

Earlier in this book some of the many of the "yeah buts," the considerations that block the path of putting technology's miracles at the service of education, were presented (see chapter 2). During the two-decade struggle to make technology part of the landscape of learning, some of the considerations voiced by educators have begun to fall away as experience has led to a better body of understanding.

A good example has to do with the subject areas deemed appropriate for the application of technology. In the beginning it was assumed that computers would be the province of math and science instruction and offer little of value elsewhere in the curriculum, but this has proven not to be the case. Technology, while having much to offer all subject areas, has proven to be of particular value in the area of literacy, an area in which all students must do well.

Other misconceptions seem to hang on more tenaciously. A classic example of this has to do with the basic skills of spelling and grammar. Those who fear the effect of computers on the young often point to spell and grammar checkers, convenience features that are included with all word processing programs, as items that represent particular problems. The argument against the use of these features with students asserts that they are crutches that will prevent youngsters from learning essential skills.

This same argument was voiced when calculators were introduced in mathematics education. Once upon a time (actually just a decade back), there was much hand wringing about allowing students to use calculators in class. Interestingly, this tempest has abated and calculator use is not only accepted but promoted. It has become a standard expectation for math programs everywhere to provide calculators to students.

It turns out that students didn't stop learning the four basic functions of arithmetic simply because calculators were handy. Furthermore, allowing them the support of calculators has allowed math educators to engage youngsters more extensively in problem solving, an enterprise that is considered more important than memorizing times tables.

The eventual acceptance of calculators has allowed us to circle back and reconsider some of the rock-solid beliefs of just a short while ago. It turns out that having youngsters memorize that 7 times 8 equals 56, that the square root of 64 is 8, and that 12 divided by 3 equals 4, wasn't such a valuable investment in time and effort after all. And finally, the educational philosophers of the early 1980s who bellowed so loudly, "What are they going to do when they're in a store and there's no calculator around to help them make change?" were wrong. After all, is there a store anywhere where calculators aren't as ubiquitous as paper?

Spell checkers promote the learning of spelling by consistently making corrections in a nonjudgmental way. The computer user must interact with the spell checker and tell it whether or not he agrees with and wants to select the correction options the checker puts in front of him. In doing so he must recognize and internalize the correction and must do so consciously. What happens frequently is that after a number of repetitions of the correction, the user learns how the word is spelled and ceases to make the mistake. Spell checkers teach spelling by helping the user spell.

WHEN IS A SCHOOL COMPUTER
NOT INSTRUCTIONAL TECHNOLOGY?

Apart from misconceptions about the place and effect of technology on instruction, there are some that belie a confusion about and discomfort with technology in general. Computers in schools make taking attendance faster and more accurate, storing and retrieving student data more efficient, and the communication between professionals and parents more effective. Technology is used to boost school security and facilitate purchasing of instructional services and materials. It is used to facilitate budgets, maintain school personnel records, and generate report cards.

In short, it has been adopted for a host of school administrative functions. As it does in any business, technology helps those charged with the business aspects of school. However, because technology is still young in its perception as a resource for teaching and learning, there sometimes exists a confusion between the two. School personnel who see the burgeoning adoption of computers to facilitate the operations end of running schools can walk away with the impression that because the school is computerized, there isn't much more to think about. How tragic it would be if this were the case, to have technology present in the school but not to bring it into the school's most core responsibility, the education of students.

Technology is frequently feared because of the danger it is perceived to pose for youngsters. Newspapers consistently run stories about youngsters lured into sexual liaisons with adults through contact made in online chat rooms. They also report the vast number of websites that feature pornography, hate messages, and dangerous information, such as instructions on how to manufacture bombs. These stories are based on actual experiences. However, withholding technology from youngsters is not wise. All of the objectionable influences that youngsters might come in contact with through technology can be accessed through other means.

We wouldn't advocate shielding youngsters from books and periodicals simply because printing has been used to produce hate material and mountains of porn. Nor would we imprison youngsters in their homes because there are bars and adult clubs in our cities where they might come in contact with unsavory individuals. Raising youngsters means supervising them. If anything, the presence of technology and the influence it has on society are reasons for adults to familiarize themselves with it, so that they may better influence youngsters in ways that they feel are appropriate.

The Internet can easily be rendered a safe, nourishing intellectual environment. There are many Internet filters available—software designed to prevent contact with objectionable websites. The federal government has mandated that schools use filtering or forfeit funding. Common home connections like AOL have built-in mechanisms that make it easy for parents to control the content that youngsters access. But preventing youngsters from using new digital technologies amounts to separating them from the world they are growing up in and in which they must learn to find their way.

LIMITLESS POSSIBILITIES THEIR PARENTS NEVER DREAMED OF

The ultimate misconception is that making technology a part of the educational experience is something that can be avoided. On the contrary, we must accept that failure to include technology is to deny a defining social and intellectual force impacting the current generation. Technology offers them inspiring activities and limitless possibilities undreamed of by their parents.

BOUND BY AN OLD, OUTMODED PARADIGM

> The ignorance of how to use new knowledge stockpiles exponentially.
>
> —Marshall McLuhan

At the beginning of the movement to bring computers into the classroom, the term "paradigm shift" was used a great deal. It isn't heard much anymore, but it ought to be resurrected. It is a perfect description of the nature and magnitude of the change that must be contended with as technology struggles to find its place in teaching and learning.

Those on the front lines of the movement to bring education into the digital age often wonder why it has been such a difficult uphill push. A principal reason is that moving from a traditional classroom to one in which twenty-first-century information skills shape the prevailing context is a paradigm shift. The school institution, unfortunately, is bound by an old, outmoded paradigm.

In the past the phrase was trotted out regularly in the sense of heady, "gee won't it be great when we get to our digital future" optimism. However, shifting paradigms is more of a gut-wrenching experience than a celebratory one. Paradigms don't shift easily. It is a high-stakes game and there are winners and losers along the sidelines. Profound change often has resistance as its close companion.

WORSHIP AT THE TEMPLE

If one listens to educators' informal sharing of reflections about their values, one thing that often comes across is their reverence for Print and The Book. To many, The Book is an almost godlike entity. For others, the very word connotes a temple where an idealized state of educational perfection called Literacy is worshiped. Along with this comes the rock-solid belief that the sole definition of "book" is a sheaf of pages sandwiched between two covers.

Educators have made the love and appreciation of The Book into the master goal of education. This is a good thing. However, a seemingly natural extension of this concept often brings educators to believe that text carried by technology, websites, and the like are not legitimate forms of content to support the study of literacy. Worse, they are seen as competing forms that seduce youngsters away from reading books, real literature, and thus become the enemy.

This well-intentioned but mushy-headed thinking is off base and ultimately very harmful. There are far more pages of text published as Web pages than there are pages of books put out every year. If we want to indoctrinate youngsters into the ways of literacy, then we should direct them to where the action is. If literacy is happening on computer monitors, then sending youngsters there is important.

Those in the publishing industry will quickly point out that without computers, most of what they do would not be possible. Writers have gravitated to technology for all aspects of their craft, from preparatory research to the process of writing itself. Their publishers use it for the production and printing of their books. It doesn't end there, though. Once published, books are sold online and advertised online; authors these days must have their own websites to promote and explain their work, as well as to further engage their audience.

Imagine an exercise in which all professional writers are separated into two groups. The writers in one group use the word processor as their primary tool. Those in the other group do not. What would the result of this experiment be? Most likely, the technology-supported writers would represent the overwhelming majority.

If professional writers—those who practice the very craft we so ardently want youngsters to understand, and whom we hope they will emulate—feel that writing in the twenty-first century involves the use of the technology, then would we want to offer youngsters an educational experience without it? Of course not! Yet adherents of the traditional paradigm of education feel comfortable doing so.

PRINT CREATURES LIVING IN A DIGITAL WORLD

In his article "Weeding: A Lament for the Loss of Books," Thomas Washington (2003), a high school librarian from Wheaton, Illinois, provides a good example of contemporary technophobic adherence to the print paradigm. He states,

> My concern is more than a nostalgic lament for a bygone era. It's not like grandma and grandpa sitting on the front stoop pining for the days of homemade ice cream. This line of thought reduces the book's demise to a matter of our apparent preference for reading on a screen instead of turning pages by hand. The issues behind my neglected book stacks are only marginally rooted in the paper vs. electronic-media debate. Yet this is as good a place as any to get a grip on the syndrome. (p. 31)

As he continues, Washington recounts an anecdote on which his thesis pivots. He describes a summer chore of "weeding" his shrinking collection of books in the high school library. Weeding is done to cull damaged and otherwise useless books from the stacks. In doing his chore he has occasion to note the pitiful level of use many of the books have been put to over the years. It seems that not only are there continually fewer and fewer books on the shelves, but the number of times they are borrowed and read have diminished dramatically as well.

He further states,

> by all appearances today's high schoolers haven't arrived at St. Francis with the same childhood wonder. Instead of books, 15 computers line our library foyer. Each station has a new, pressed-wood tabletop and tilt chairs, a kind of Starship Enterprise command post from which students navigate their way along the information Autobahn. Installing computers in this high school library has had the same ruinous effect as television in the home. Think. What the TV did to conversation around the family dinner table, the computer has done to extended bouts of concentration. Students "surf" the Internet, meaning that the longer they stand on top of the waves of information, the better the ride. The goal is never to go under, never to fully immerse oneself in the contents of the page. (p. 31)

If Washington had made an effort to see the deep connection that now exists between the world of books and the realm of online text-based content, he would understand that there exists no conflict between the two. In fact, the resources currently online augment, support, and promote the appreciation and understanding of books. One startling example of this is the extensive website of Scholastic, one of the most successful companies ever to enter the arena of publishing books for youngsters.

Among the many things to be found in the Scholastic site is a clear example of how technology offers a greatly enhanced platform on which youngsters may come to understand and love books. This is the Writing with Writers section. Here, the same authors that youngsters may have read establish interfaces through which a more in-depth relationship, author to reader, may be established and savored.

This goes far beyond the usual author websites found in abundance on the Web. In the Writing with Writers section, authors discuss the genre within which they work, tell their own personal history explaining why they write and how they wrote the works being focused on. In some instances there may be an opportunity to be in direct contact with the author through the use of e-mail.

One exceptional opportunity is to be found in the area devoted to myths (among others). Here, the author invites her readers to use what they have learned from the exercises she has provided illuminating the dimensions of the genre and to write their own work within it. But the interactive nature of the site goes deeper. At the conclusion of writing, the students may submit their writing to be published on the site. And here we come to an example of one of the most profound changes in the realm of student opportunity that the technology has brought about.

Publishing has long been considered the final, culminating phase of the writing process. Most frequently it has been hampered by minimal opportunities for students to engage in an activity that in our modern, media-driven world would really be considered publishing. It is hard for today's sophisticated youngsters to see recopying their work in a *final* clean version with ballpoint on lined notebook paper as publishing. Placing such work on a hallway bulletin board hardly can be construed as being published.

Student work that appears on the Scholastic website can be made to appear every bit as polished as the work published by the professional authors who are featured there. But there is a remarkable further dimension to what can be accessed on this site. Not only does the site publish the work of youngsters (this is free and open to all, by the way), but the author who invited the youngster to write and publish in the first place will critique the work as well, bring the cycle of writing, reading, reflecting, responding, and writing again full circle.

Let's encourage the Washingtons of the world to put their lamentation of the loss of The Book as a form aside long enough to investigate how today's information technology is actually preserving and venerating the form in a natural and effective manner.

This high school librarian's article concludes, "In this era of specialization and high productivity, books and literature remain the great potential integrators, the glue that can repair technology's arrogant muscling in between the stacks" (p. 31). Yes, but they can do that even better when empowered by those aspects of technology-carried content that have been lavishly and lovingly crafted to support them in these functions.

That row of fifteen computers is not the enemy. It represents a literacy-friendly development and the shape of things to come. Embrace it!

PRINT PREJUDICE

Shifting the paradigm to include technology resources as legitimate and valuable for teaching literacy is a struggle because of the way in which print traditionalists achieved overwhelming dominance in education. As an outgrowth of the long history of text domination in our schools, there has been a Darwinian-type evolution alongside it of print-prejudiced educators. Generation after generation, individuals who have thrived in the print-based intellectual environment of our schools have picked up the torch to run classrooms for the next generation. The result is a cohort of educators who do not grasp the legitimacy and value of digital text.

Multiple intelligences advocates, like Howard Gardner, theorize that traditional schooling was developed around a limited set of intelligences, particularly those relating to learning in a print-dominant program. If we understand the school institution as a sort of intellectual ecosystem, it becomes clear that what has evolved is a culture that is very attached to maintaining the dominance of print.

Those who have thrived in the print-ruled world of yesterday are today's teachers and principals. Consciously or not, they perpetuate a brand of learning that promotes print dominance and seeks to exclude manifestations of technology-supported literacy.

A NEW SOURCE OF INTELLECTUAL NOURISHMENT

We have come to a crucial crossroad in the future of education. An important new source of intellectual nourishment has appeared. In many ways its components are the same as the traditional: chains of letters that conform to rules of grammar and syntax. However, this new source is accessed differently. Instead of sitting statically on piles of paper, literature now moves dynamically across cathode ray tubes and plasma monitors. It dances at dizzying speeds and interacts with the creatures who create and consume it.

Through the emergence of such manifestations of technology as on-screen text, the intellectual environment has become richer and better able to support intelligent life. Educators need only to adapt to this change in order to thrive. In doing so they will be better nourishing the next generation.

BREAKING WITH THE SEQUENCE

In his article "A Taxonomy Is Not a Sequence," Chris M. Worsnop, author of *Screening Images: Ideas for Media Education,* makes the point that in their use of one of education's greatest cornerstones, the majority of educators make a dangerous and mushy-headed leap of understanding. He gives the ever-enlightening, and ever-revered concept of Bloom's taxonomy its due respect and praise, but points out that because it is so unchallenged, misinterpreting the correct way to apply it is the cause of much mischief.

What's interesting from the point of view of trying to understand the resistance to technology adoption by our teachers is that the validity and brilliance of the taxonomy itself is not called into question in the piece; rather, that an outmoded paradigm for learning, and hence, teaching, renders this perennial piece of education school wisdom counterproductive. That paradigm, or more accurately, piece of the larger paradigm of traditional print-based education, is the until recently unchallenged belief that learning occurs in a straight line.

Truly, the belief goes further, embodying the notion that in addition to learning, even perceiving as well as using content, are inherently and thoroughly part of a linear experience.

In the article, Worsnop wisely uses a *killer app* of examples, the way that software users learn new pieces of software. If one were to follow the traditional interpretation of Bloom's taxonomy and attempt to teach a new piece of software, one would insist that students use the manual and that they progress through it in linear fashion, not moving from point A to point B until significant proficiency, perhaps mastery, has been achieved. The idea of moving from point A to point C would be unsettlingly out of the question. This rock-solid belief set, by the way, pretty much rules the entire public school landscape, defining education for hundreds of millions of youngsters.

But Worsnop points out that we have long since discovered that one doesn't use the software manual in this fashion. In fact, one doesn't use it at all. It is pretty much a universally accepted insider joke among computer users that the manual is put on a shelf somewhere or thrown in the trash. This is so much the case that numerous software publishers no longer provide printed manuals but rather websites or downloadable manuals for those rarer instances in which a user actually needs or wants them.

So how does the new user learn his software? He jumps in and tries things, experiments, draws conclusions, follows his nose, his successes, the software itself, draws inferences from other software that seems similar, and on and on. In other words, in a totally nonlinear fashion.

The correct understanding of Bloom's taxonomy is that it is a listing, a hierarchy of types of learning, of intellectual growth states. It is not a prescription for a series of steps that must be followed sequentially for learning to occur. Despite the widespread misinterpretation of Bloom's great idea, experience with the learning of technology proves that this is not the case! What's startling about this example is that it is so obviously, incontestably true for almost everyone. Even though it so clearly disproves the linear learning myth, teachers, even software-using teachers who should doubt the old paradigm, continue to cling to it.

The traditional paradigm which asserts that learning, knowing, and processing information is inherently linear in nature lies behind teacher techno-resistance. One simply can't exist as an intellectual being in the new nonlinear paradigm and continue to function in the old one.

CONCEIVING A TECHNOLOGY-SUPPORTED EDUCATION

Chapter 2 included illustrations about how technology can support, in new and powerful ways, teaching and learning from the point of view of traditional schooling. In other words, How does technology impact the traditional subjects taught in school?

Technology adaptations that support the traditional are a good start. More importantly, though, they serve as an entry point into the realm of using technology for teaching and learning. A realm in which educators can go beyond simple adaptation and create things that are nontraditional, where they can explore. It is a common and very unfortunate misconception that technology's principal contribution is to make the traditional teaching of traditional subjects more effective. There is so much more to discover.

There are other ways that technology changes teaching and learning and these may prove to be of far greater importance. There are other contexts for instruction that it establishes. Interestingly, some of these, like collaborative learning, are "reform" items that have been pursued for a long time without an appropriate concrete vehicle for implementation presenting itself. Others, like research, are traditional items that have been around for years as a goal of instruction, but without there ever being a solid platform from which to conduct them. Technology is changing both.

WAYS THAT TECHNOLOGY TAKES LEARNING INTO NEW AND RECLAIMED TERRITORY

Authentic Activities

For most of human history, education was accomplished not through school but through some form of apprenticeship. Perhaps it was simply working on the family farm or perhaps something more elaborate, like a formal apprenticeship to a craftsman, banker, or doctor. The commonality between all of these is that the student learned by doing real things, for a real purpose, in the real world.

With the advent of school this changed. At school, students are traditionally given tasks to perform by the teacher. These tasks, while perhaps well designed from the abstract cognitive growth point of view, are most often divorced from the real world. Consequently, it is difficult for students to see or experience relevance. Many of the tasks have little to do with actual products or services in the real world. Much of what is done in school is directed by notions that knowledge, such as calculus, is good for its own sake. It isn't taught to prepare students for actual application with real consequences.

In traditional schools, furthermore, youngsters must study and learn what a teacher prescribes for them, when she prescribes it. But in our culture, with its ever-deepening desire for individual freedom, this is unacceptable to a great portion of the population. Technology, because it can provide so much information and generate so many customized versions of it, can help establish a learning environment in which learners are allowed to follow their own instincts, interests, and passions without turning their back on basic principles and concepts of learning.

A good example of authentic learning activities are online projects like Journey North. In these, students from throughout North America assist scientists in tracking the movements of migratory species. The students, for instance, collect data by observing and counting migrating birds. Then they use the Internet to report their local findings which, in turn, become part of a mass study. The project couldn't work without the contributions of thousands of local data collectors. Participation in these projects is authentic, real work. It produces a real effect, in the real world.

To take this a step further, youngsters may wish to participate by tracking a species or behavior that captures their personal interest. So, an individual may be participating in a general class project, but doing so in a self-defined, personal way.

Student Publishing

A similar concept or perhaps the killer application of authentic activities has to do with student publishing. This is as core an activity as possible in today's education, as all youngsters must learn to write. Hands down, the preferred approach to the teaching and learning of writing is the writing process, a formalized approach in which young writers are guided through a series of conceptualized stages. The culminating phase is publishing, the logical conclusion of numerous other stages that involve prewriting, drafting, and revising.

Many educators find that creating a finished product which students can truly accept as a "published" version of their work has been a challenge. But with current digital technologies teachers and students can have access to the same media tools that professional publishing houses use as they prepare books for press. Personal computers, word processing, desktop publishing, low-cost color inkjet printers, scanners, digital cameras, and the like have turned everyman's office and every teacher's classroom into a potential publishing house capable of putting out polished products. This is so much the case that often it would take a professional eye to distinguish student work from commercial product.

However, the power of the technology to transform student publishing goes much further. Exercising one's voice becomes meaningful when there is an audience to hear it. Student work that is published on the Internet is placed in an arena where an endless number of audience members may see and appreciate it. By getting one's site listed with various search engines or by sending out e-mail with a description of the student writing and an embedded hyperlink to the Web page that bears it, one can guarantee with a reasonable degree of certainty that the voice of the writer will be heard.

Research

Educators have always wanted to engage youngsters in activities that can be called research. This has been extremely difficult to achieve, though, because of the isolation of the classroom. How does one learn about navigating the vast repositories of information our libraries represent without access to those libraries? Yes, one can talk about techniques in finding items buried in the vast stacks of hard copy books at a nearby library (assuming there is one nearby) but such activities are largely doomed to fall flat on their face. There is no way to make this relevant by simply talking about it.

Lamentably, in our schools "research" rarely amounts to more than leafing through two or three popular encyclopedias. Yes, in using these, students easily discover entries for their topics organized alphabetically, but only if one's query for information is not too far-fetched. Unfortunately, the encyclopedia gives them only short, predigested pieces that can be easily paraphrased and turned in as one's own "research." Little about true research is learned. Worst of all, everyone's research seems nearly identical.

The World Wide Web, a vast archive of data and opinion, is easily accessed at school. While search engine and browser technology enable the work, it is necessary to understand the nature and rules of research in order to carry it out. Technology makes true research something that can be part of every student's education. It also makes it a creative and exciting experience.

Modeling, Illustrating, Simulations

Some things are just better understood when they are seen. Words, although essential, are not always sufficient to illustrate new concepts to youngsters. The Web is a perfect medium for serving up a mixture of illustrative graphics and text. Beyond simple drawings or photos, websites are often rich in animations as well.

The simulations found on websites are often interactive, requiring students to manipulate them in order to complete an activity. A buoyancy simulation, for instance, may require the student user to predict how high a given vessel will ride in a liquid medium and then give feedback on the accuracy of his estimation by showing the actual level it assumes through an animated series of drawings, or a youngster may get a seemingly real look at earth from nine miles out in space as he navigates a space vehicle; or any of a wide variety of virtual math manipulatives may give concrete, three-dimensional reality to the behavior of numbers.

Collaborative Learning

We've moved away from the old model of the teacher as owner of knowledge, a commodity with which he fills the empty vessel of his students' minds. Much thought has gone into the social aspects of learning and their role in the construction of knowledge and meaning. Part of this newly understood context is the understanding that youngsters can have a better experience of learning if they do so in partnership with peers.

On a practical level, though, teachers feel hard-pressed to make this wonderful concept come alive in their classrooms. Technology has serendipitously facilitated this approach.

Good examples are to be found in instructional software. One in particular is the model established by Tom Snyder Productions. Rain Forest Researchers (and others of their titles), provides youngsters with challenges to complete as the focus of their studies. The students become part of a team in which they each play a vital role. They must do their part in order for their team to compete against others. They must utilize what they learn and their judgment as they solve problems and create solutions. The technology guides them through a controlled experience in ways that would be hard to duplicate otherwise.

Other examples of technology-facilitated collaboration are broader. Youngsters' work is posted online for peers to review and learn from. Posted book reports are a common form of this. There are also many opportunities for classes to work together on projects across great distances.

The Stevens Institute of Technology's Center for Improved Engineering and Science Education's (CIESE) online Asteroid Watch: Fireballs from the Sky project is a good example. The project website (www.k12science.org/asteroidwatch/) states, "Have you ever looked up in the sky and seen a shooting star? Have you ever wondered what would happen if such a 'star' ever decided to head towards Earth and was big enough to threaten us? . . . This project will help you to answer these and other questions. It will also get you involved in collaborating with other schools around the world in determining factors affecting the appearance of impact craters and their ejecta [Matter ejected; material thrown out; as, the ejecta of a volcano; the ejecta, or excreta, of the body]." The project is made possible by the focused use of several types of common technology applications.

Another example is the National Math Trail. The website (www .nationalmathtrail.org/) explains,

The National Math Trail is an opportunity for K–12 teachers and students to discover and share the math that exists in their own environments. Students explore their communities and create one or more math problems that relate to what they find. Teachers submit the problems to the National Math Trail site, along with photos, drawings, sound recordings, and videos—whatever can be adapted to the Internet. All submissions will be posted to the site as they are submitted. They are also indexed according to grade level and math topic and will remain on the site for access by educators, students and parents.

Connecting to Experts and Mentors

Our technologically connected world makes it possible for young people to learn from more adults than ever before. Shouldn't we to take advantage of this possibility? Many websites make it possible for youngsters to interact with an adult who is a master or expert at something. Such interactions can result in a rich educational experience.

The PITSCO Ask an Expert site (www.pitsco.com/Resources/resframe.htm) enables youngsters to e-mail questions to any of dozens and dozens of experts. Experts made available through this site range from computer scientists to composers to journalists to auto mechanics.

Refdesk.com has a similar site with over seventy experts ranging from whale scientists to accountants. Drexel University's Dr. Math (www.mathforum.org/dr.math/) can be e-mailed questions pertaining to mathematics. AskMayo, a website from the Mayo clinic, will post answers to medical questions e-mailed in. The All Experts website (www.mayoclinic.com/findinformation/answers/index.cfm) has over 3,500 experts on tap.

Another example of this wonderful type of resource is Mentor Place (www.mentorplace.org/login.do), created through a partnership of IBM and EdReach. Here, though, ongoing relationships take the place of one-shot questions and answers.

Online homework help sites have become a common type of technology-based support for youngsters. Some of them, like the Achievement Advocate Online Mentoring Community (www.achievementadvocate.org/), provide a deep level of ongoing support.

Another dimension is represented by the Wings website (http://wings.utexas.org/about.html) from the University of Texas School of Education. On this site master teachers from throughout Texas engage in long-term mentor/mentee relationships. The intention of the program is to utilize technology to provide a better level of support for new teachers than could be provided otherwise.

Individualized Instruction

This is another holy grail of education that has been very difficult to achieve. With thirty youngsters and one teacher to a class making up our historical average, we have, out of necessity, largely developed a sink-or-swim reality in the classroom. Keep up with the group or you're sunk.

The software titles that help solve this problem are too numerous to name. Basically, they harness the computer's processing, sorting, and archiving capabilities (its strong suits) making certain types of individualized instruction easy to achieve. Youngsters are presented with content, be it text, multimedia, interactive, or whatever. Periodically they are fed questions.

In a traditional classroom, after wrong answers are discussed briefly, it is time for the class to move on. Time is precious, so no wonder performance levels are so low.

Not with instructional software, though. The computer keeps redirecting the student to the same type of question that he is getting wrong. It adjusts the level of the question to meet his level of competence and interjects supplementary bits of information and explanation as the database drills down to specific weaknesses in understanding. Or it directs him back to where he was last doing well, enabling him to address the source of his problem. The computer is tireless and if done properly, the software is loaded with a great many variations of each type of question.

Not all learning has to do with basic facts and skills. Open-ended, self-directed inquiry experiences are wonderful for students. Unfortunately, the amount of content that a classroom or even a school library can afford a youngster who would like to follow his own instincts and passions in deciding what to study is limited. With the World Wide Web, a vast, virtually inexhaustible library is a mouse click away. A class of thirty can now have the luxury of all students working on a different topic without stretching the limits of teacher, classroom, or resources, a great step forward for the developing intellect.

Adaptive and Assistive Technology

Nineteenth-century U.S. citizens facing the challenge of emigrating to the untamed West had a favorite saying: "God made man, but Sam Colt made men equal." The six-shooter, a technological innovation of the time, allowed all to compete and participate on a more level playing field. Individuals who would never have faced danger without their Colt equalizer went forth and settled the western half of our nation.

Today, there are a raft of technology innovations that can even the score for many youngsters who are challenged in their educational participation. Word processors that read text out loud aid the visually impaired. Braille computers allow the blind to benefit from the writing support of word processing programs. Touch screen monitors and devices like the "head mouse" allow students with impaired movement to participate. Nonverbal youngsters are supported by programs that talk or play back prerecorded messages for them. Those with intellectual impairments can go further than ever before. Word processing–style programs facilitate for them critical reading factors such as word prediction. Specialists have even noticed that autistic students benefit from computer programs that support them in having increased focus on tasks.

Multiple Intelligences

On a similar note, followers of educational theorist Howard Gardner recognize that school traditionally favors individuals who relate well to print and verbally dominated learning. It excludes a great many other students.

Gardner's theory holds that there are at least eight intelligences: linguistic, musical, logical-mathematical, spatial, bodily kinesthetic, interpersonal, intrapersonal, and naturalist. Individuals show strengths in some of them or in combinations of a few.

Technology brings such a wide variety of learning experiences to the classroom that individuals have a far greater chance of having their particular intelligences addressed. The interactive, animated nature of much software makes this so, as does the increased opportunity of human interaction created by telecommunications applications.

Motivation and Engagement

In recent years education has established a standards-based approach to instruction. Groups of experts have established lists of competencies in an effort to define what students should know and be able to do when they exit school. The testing and accountability movement likewise, attempts to make certain that such competencies are actually learned.

While these efforts are unimpeachable theoretically, do they in fact make a difference in the intellectual lives of students? Young minds need to be stimulated. The new technologies can help educators engage youngsters in relevant and exciting activities. Content, delivered by software, has the look and feel that the video game generation has come to expect of anything purporting to be worthy of its attention.

Interactivity and individualization have become prerequisites to engage our youth. The social aspects of learning facilitated through telecommunications make technology essential, as do opportunities for self-directed learning that the vast warehouse of content on the Web makes possible.

Because today's youth is maturing in a technologically shaped world, its education must reflect the profound influence of those technologies. The sooner adults who are addressing the issue of educating the digital generation accept this, the sooner education will get itself back on track.

INTEGRATION: TECHNOLOGY'S KILLER MISSTEP

Anyone who's been around schools for the past decade or so has probably heard the term "technology integration" used over and over. The term means to infuse or weave technology into the general instructional program. Unfortunately, it has also picked up a connotation of being very difficult to do.

This is not the case. Technology need not represent a difficult set of resources for educators to take advantage of. Most unfortunately, technology integration's reputation for difficulty precedes it and often discourages educators from attempting implementation. It also has become a self-fulfilling prophecy, with educators finding difficulty that they have been led to expect. This is sometimes fueled by service providers who sell professional development programs. By accentuating the difficult, they create additional need that more of their service will satisfy.

In reality, the technology is easy to use and its integration into teaching and learning can be natural and fluid, unless prospective users impose or project a feared difficulty. We need to distance ourselves from "technology integration" as a Sisyphean burden and adopt the idea of technology use as the productive, joyful experience many educators have discovered it to be.

Technology integration is simultaneously a key concept and a bogus one. It's key, if by integration we mean using technology in such a way that it becomes part of the fabric of teaching and learning and not a technology course end unto itself. If approached this way, before long it will become transparent, part of the background of daily work.

Integration becomes a bogus concept when its name conjures up a Mount Everest to climb, a lofty but impossible dream. Integration, when stated as a Herculean goal becomes one. It consumes resources, time, and effort. Few of today's educational "goals" are ever achieved in good measure and technology integration is no different.

In large measure technology is always aimed at producing increased results through diminished effort. Technologies like the tractor, the automobile, and the calculator are all examples of human ingenuity making work easier. We might define technology as humankind's effort to increase productivity while decreasing toil. It is ironic, therefore, that "technology integration" has for so many become synonymous with something hard to attain, something that requires great effort. In this sense, technology integration is not a goal worthy of the efforts of teachers and students.

ACOT FOR THE FEW: TECH TO GO FOR THE MANY

Between 1985 and 1998 Apple Computer sponsored one of the best-known experiments in tracking the establishment and stickiness of putting computers in the classroom. This program was called ACOT (Apple Classrooms of Tomorrow).

As an outgrowth of the ACOT work, a well-known and widely disseminated concept of how teachers come to use technology was developed. The ACOT model holds that teachers slowly evolve through five distinct phases: entry, adoption, adaptation, appropriation, and finally invention. While this may be a useful model for understanding teachers in the process of becoming technology users, it is not one for making this shift take place. Implicit in the ACOT model is the understanding that technology adoption by educators is long, slow, labor-intensive, expensive, and difficult to achieve. This is no longer a productive understanding.

Digital technology is designed to be easy to use. It is conceived to shadow its previous, nondigital corollaries, creating easy-to-understand parallels between the digital and real world. A good example of this can be seen in the move from DOS era, text-based operating systems to the graphic user interface of the Mac operating system.

Understanding computers and comprehending how they dovetailed to the reality of the office was quite difficult in the early years of the PC. Few folks were comfortable in using a computer other than in a very prescribed formulaic manner. It was generally acknowledged that the realm of computers was either for techno-confident geeks who were comfortable in such an artificial dimension, or the province of secretaries, hapless office drones who had no choice but to tough it out.

With the advent of the first popular GUI (graphic user interface), the selling point of the new Macintosh line of computers, this was no longer so. Now, instead of doing one's work in the undefined, incomprehensible, new reality of the computer, one had a virtual desktop. This new space, one that mirrored the traditional office, was replete with files, folders, trash can, and on and on. With the GUI it isn't difficult to understand how to generate and manage files using such a system. All this is because a good deal of intelligent, creative effort was put into making it easy.

This is not true for all technologies, though. Automobiles have become more difficult to maintain and repair. Their designers and manufacturers have no motivation to make these things easy. They know that the consumer will turn to a trained professional for repairs who will equip and prepare himself to handle this function. The increasing complexity of cars improves and reinforces his value as a service provider, and the consumer accepts this.

But for education, technology *must* be conceived of as *easy* to use! The rank and file of educators will only fully make the shift into the broad-based adoption of technology for instruction if they see doing so as easy. This is the only type of adoption that makes sense or can possibly succeed.

This is all the more true because of another often-missed aspect of technology: value through ubiquity. Without the presence of a critical mass of teachers using technology, it will continue to be relegated to the status of novelty. Think about e-mail. Its value is obvious because everyone uses it. If just a few folks used it, it would be, at best, an oddity.

Of course, if one is looking for examples of difficult things to do in using technology, even things that a teacher might engage in, it is not difficult to find them. On the other hand, the most common uses of the technology—surfing the Web, simple word processing, and the production of the type of charts and graphs called for in the world of education, simple presentation functions like PowerPoint, e-mail—are all very easy to use and in a sense require little effort to learn.

PUTTING A MAGNIFYING GLASS
ON TEACHING AND IMPROVING IT

If the technology itself doesn't require much learning, then what is it that teachers need to learn in order to take advantage of the mother lode of technology-supported teaching resources out there? What they need to learn are better approaches to *teaching*.

Teachers are not taking advantage of the plethora of Web-based resources available not so much because of their unfamiliarity with technology skills, but because they are not comfortable, in general, with adopting any type of new resource and adapting it to classroom use. The technology skills are just a small part of the picture, as is tech support.

Teachers will take advantage of a given resource if they understand its advantages, and that doing so will not be disruptive. We are encountering resistance largely because a requisite number of practitioners have not been encouraged to experiment in this realm. A sufficient amount of demystification, confidence that this is a low-risk activity, and encouragement has not been given by supervisors.

Could it be that the slow adoption of technology speaks more to the poor state of preparedness of teachers in the quicksilver milieu of ever-shifting goals, methods, and resources of the new information age, than it does about the appropriateness of that technology for use in teaching and learning? Isn't the paucity of good practice evidenced in using the recently arrived technologies an opportunity to put a magnifying glass on teaching and improve it?

TEACHERLESS CLASSROOMS:
THE FLESH-AND-BLOOD DIVIDE?

Teacherless classrooms? This feared outcome of the technology revolution is possible to a degree. But it won't be the technology that precipitates it. The value our society puts on teachers and education will be the key determinants.

A few years back, an entrepreneur put out a startling application of technology for the classroom. This company made arrangements to have Nobel Prize winners present lectures through its pay subscription website employing on-demand digital video. As a follow-up, the famous lecturers were available to classes to answer questions through e-mail. As startling and brilliant as this piece appears, it opened up the door for one of instructional technology's thornier issues.

As an unfortunate result of the remarkable value offered in having Nelson Mandela, for instance, teach political science coursework, the consumer is likely to conclude that, at least conceptually, Mandela is a far more highly qualified, more inspiring teacher than most real (read: licensed) teachers. Even though it is for a lofty goal, this service involves replacing the teacher with a technology solution. Add to that the fact that this teaching is much less expensive to provide than that provided by a flesh-and-blood teacher, and you have opened the lid to Pandora's box. Or have you?

The saving grace is that this piece would be implemented best if the class on the receiving end had the opportunity to digest, reflect on, and respond to the content through the talents of a teacher capable of mediating its out-of-the-box format. In such a scenario there is a win/win situation: improved content and delivery for learners and a new and valued role for the teacher.

As extreme as this example may be, it points out one very compelling way that technology may be used to either improve or degrade the role of the teacher. Depending on its implementation, technology may either increase the need for a good teacher, or eliminate that need. If an accomplished teacher can be brought over the Internet into a classroom that does not have a highly effective one, or one of equal quality, how will this affect our motivation to improve the profession and bring more and better folks into it? Perhaps we are heading not for a digital divide but just the opposite. Perhaps, as it becomes clear that quality presentation of content can be bought cheaply and with consistent quality, from the tech companies, we will end up with a flesh-and-blood divide!

MEDIATOR OF THE TECHNOLOGY: A NEW ROLE FOR TEACHERS

Teachers and those who write about teaching, often talk about the "joys of teaching," "the teachable moment," and the occasional prickly sensation on the back of one's neck when an antagonistic student accepts the help of a teacher or when a group of students volunteer to work after school on a project. Between teachers and students, emotional and intellectual exchanges occur. Trust and affection evolve into life-long, cross-generational friendships. These relationships are deeply satisfying to teachers. They are, in Dan Lorrtie's words, the psychic rewards of teaching.

—Larry Cuban, *Oversold and Underused*, p. 169

To use technology properly in teaching and learning calls for teachers having a new and reinvigorated role.

It's already become a cliché that through the use of technology the teacher's role will morph from "the sage on the stage to the guide on the side." But that doesn't leave the teacher in a very good place. Being a guide on the side is not a very inspiring or inspired place to be. Teachers inherently want a more active more central role without resorting to a completely teacher-centered approach to instruction.

It's also true that youngsters gravitate toward the maturity and confidence of an adult who is an experienced learner without the imposition of teacher-centered focuses. Where this leaves us is with a new and third role of the teacher in the information age. In the digital classroom teachers will become the mediator of the technology.

It is through the teacher's experience, competence, and expertise as a learner that the technology begins to take on meaning, at least for a good part of what can be done with technology in the classroom.

In order to ensure that a rich, well-balanced, learning experience is what youngsters receive, there must be a teacher present who is a confident, mature learner and who will mediate the experience of technology use. This is far more significant than merely knowing and handling the technology. Mediating has to do with sophistication in the ways of knowledge and learning. Particularly in the ways that technology impacts and has changed the learning paradigm. And sophistication in the ways that it has not.

This understanding doesn't invalidate all those educational uses of technology in which students sit isolated and immersed in the reality of their personal terminals. Such experiences offer great value if youngsters are prepared for them and debriefed afterward by a teacher. As mediator, the teacher represents a kind of home base, a source of wisdom to return to after exploring on one's own. As mediator the teacher functions as a learning sounding board and coach to help sort it all out.

In all probability, though, it is the overlooked modality of technology for group instruction that will figure most highly in establishing comfort in its value for teaching. Think about the way people respond to the campfire or the hearth or the radio or the television. Those things are central to what it means to be a human being.

In the early days, its golden age, television supported the family instead of dividing it. Families owned a single television and gathered around it each evening sharing the experience of getting content through the cathode ray tube. They would reflect on and discuss, debate, argue, whatever, but they would communally share in the experience.

In many schools that have deployed technology this shared experience is what's missing. The impulse seems to have been to march youngsters down to the lab and to have them each confront and interact with their own, individual screen. Yes, perhaps in doing so they take advantage of the extraordinary opportunities for individualized instruction that the technology offers, but they also turn their back on the social learning that comes from group technology use.

Discussion and debate is central to the higher goals of education. Defending ideas and beliefs through accountable talk, relating and retelling what's been learned to peers, giving and receiving feedback and having work corrected, acknowledged, and processed by the group are all valuable. Human communication and interaction are essential needs for young people. Technology-using educators need to include them.

Acting as the technology mediator, teachers can impact core literacy learning activities. Rose Reissman of Long Island University, an expert in literacy instruction, has done much work concerning student appreciation of the book, particularly how technology can be brought into play most effectively to impact literacy when employed properly.

She describes a scenario in which the classroom technology deployment would involve a single computer projecting an image for the whole group to see by means of an LCD projector or large screen monitor. The result would be something of a digital big book. In presenting books to youngsters, particularly picture books, the big book is a highly beloved format for early grades. Using it often involves a series of prereading activities that the teacher leads. For instance, there is the "book walk" in which the teacher presents and discusses the pages and illustrations of the book to the students before actual work on reading it begins.

Some teachers use technology to support this by scanning the pictures and importing them into a presentation software, such as Power-Point. Then they can do a graphically and visually rich presentation to the class. It is accompanied by the very large format images of a digital slide show, establishing a somewhat environmental context for the book being studied. None of this requires sophisticated technology, just low-cost office applications that are easy to use. Moreover, the cost of the projector or large-screen monitor is about the same as a computer. So, for the cost of only two computers, an experience that is more appropriate and engaging for this type of learning can be accomplished at a price far lower than that of an entire lab.

One valuable technology-supported instructional resource in particular that cries out for teacher mediation is the author website, which most authors have. Young people's authors lavish attention and affection on their sites and make them highly personal. They use them to communicate the special and endearing aspects of their art to their young audiences.

It is problematic though to go from whole group instruction, common in literacy instruction, to sending the students to a lab for the technology-supported portion of the lesson. In the lab students are often isolated socially and intellectually. This may even be counterproductive educationally. Far better to have the group encounter the author's website together in a group discussion format. Again, an expensive and hard-to-come-by lab is no longer needed for a valuable set of instructional activities.

A good example of an author website, one that represents free content available to enrich core literacy studies, is the website of Sandra Cisneros. She is a very popular author whose works are used widely in schools. One of her books, *The House on Mango Street*, has over the past few years proven to be one of the most popular works to be read in our middle and high school classrooms. The second chapter in the book, "Hairs," was later adapted by the author herself as a picture book for younger students called *Pelitos* (Spanish for hairs).

Youngsters are quite familiar with Cisneros's work. And it is natural for them, as they grow to love her works, to develop a curiosity, enthusiasm, and affection for her. This is something they experience with all of their favorite authors. They want to learn about their lives, why they write, and the other things they do. They hold authors to be very special people.

Cisneros's website is designed to engage youngsters. On entering, they find an entire world to be explored. There are many paths into this world, all of them relating to the themes of her books. One path in particular, that of the book *Pelitos,* is very special, offering magical things to discover. Click on the image of the cover of *Pelitos* and you activate Web buttons, interactive items for young explorers.

In *The House on Mango Street,* Cisneros describes a rich, multitextured culture of Mexican Americans living in her neighborhood in urban Chicago. The website's buttons relate to that culture. Activate them and up come crowing roosters and icons of the Virgin of Guadeloupe, church bells, and even vocabulary cards with words in Spanish to be learned. This is precisely the type of experience that is best moderated by the teacher for the youngsters. Not so much because of technology experience, but more importantly because she is an experienced learner, a navigator of life and its surprises and opportunities.

SOFTWARE TO MEET THE MEDIATION ROLE OF TEACHERS

Unfortunately a great deal of instructional software that is put on the market, including titles that on many levels are truly wonderful, are put out without an understanding of the need for group confrontation of content that is mediated for students. Software is sometimes produced and sold without regard to where and how it will be deployed. Whether it will be installed for use in a single computer, a grouping of four to six computers, or for that matter, a full thirty work station lab, or even an entire school seems not to matter to some publishers. But the dynamics of use ought to be taken into account. The experience of a student working individually with software is very different from that of a class exploring and discussing it with a teacher who is astute in the ways to take advantage of it to support learning.

One company that has produced software that shows a good understanding of the social dynamics in the use of technology is Tom Snyder Productions. It has put out some startling examples of software that accounts for and takes advantages of them. The original motivation for their design approach was an accommodation of the fact that in a previous era schools couldn't afford to put more than one computer in a classroom. Serendipitously, however, now that many more computers are available, the groundbreaking work of Tom Snyder is just as relevant, if not more so. The format that this group developed offers an approach to get us beyond the pitfall of the isolating effect that one to one ratios of students to computers may have.

One series of titles that illustrates this approach is Decisions, Decisions. This software presents groups of youngsters with problems of, for example, a political or environmental nature. A great deal of thinking and reflection is required from students as they work toward a decision. The software fosters friendly, collegial competition between groups, allowing for whole-class, multiteam, and single-team use.

The students confront the software as a group, discuss the problem they have been presented with, and drill down to practical decision-making configurations. These are reflected on and compared to that of other groups.

What's particularly wonderful about this format is that an entire class can be given a very rich experience that is driven by a single computer. Perhaps more attention put into designing great software for instruction will produce better educational results than simply acquiring more computer hardware.

NO NEED TO BE A GEEK

In order to encourage teachers to assume the role of technology mediator they, and those who supervise them, need to understand that they need not be expert in the use of technology itself.

But is it reasonable to assume that the average teacher can take on this role? In order to take advantage of *entry-level* technology, a teacher needs to know how to (1) read and reflect, something that is central to the spirit and culture of teaching, (2) follow directions, something even more aligned with the spirit of schooling, and (3) click a mouse. There is little more to learn in order to begin using technology as a resource for teaching and learning. What do those guys in Silicon Valley lay awake at night thinking about? Simple: making money, of course, and more precisely, making money by making technology so simple to use that everyone will want to buy it.

Furthermore, it is already a cliché that in today's classes it is common to find youngsters, especially those with access to computers at home, who know more about technology than the teacher does. Those students are a wonderful and appropriate source of technical expertise and can relieve the teacher of this responsibility as she concentrates on teaching and learning. The role of the mediator has little to do with being an accomplished tech geek and everything to do with sophistication in the dynamics of learning and of group work.

FROM SAGE TO GUIDE TO SHAMAN

Yes, the teacher is no longer the sage on the stage, but he's not the guide on the side, either. The role of the technology-mediating teacher is more like that of a tribal shaman or campfire leader. Campfire leader was truly an important, satisfying role back when the campfire was an all-important social ritual, when it was the preeminent technology of the day.

Another piece of the truth in this can be seen in the experience of Bob, a high school vocational education teacher in a small Massachusetts city. Bob, who teaches auto shop, has logged many years of success with youngsters whose bent is not particularly academic in nature.

In preparing his young charges for what can be a successful career as a mechanic or auto body specialist, he also coaches them through core academic subjects. He works hard to help them pass required tests and exit their school experience with a diploma in hand. It is for this reason that when the school district decided to acquire a highly motivational and interactive piece of software entitled Destination Math (Riverdeep software), it decided to place this new resource in the vocational education department for Bob to use.

Interestingly, the computer deployment model in use featured a full-blown computer lab within a few feet of Bob's shop. His instincts, however, told him that with the population of students he was working with, the lab approach would not be wise. Breaking with convention and with the intended restrictions of the very design of the instructional technology environment made available to him, Bob opted to present Destination Math as whole group instruction.

Even though a layout of the computer lab was designed to isolate youngsters by placing them at individual workstations, Bob's insights into the dynamics of working with easily distracted adolescents told him to redirect the flow of attention. He modified the situation and used the software to fuel lessons that were large group discussions in format. He turned the use of the software into a communal activity, an off-the-cuff left turn that made a world of difference.

The result of this was a smashing success. Bob's class stayed on task. The youngsters learned material that they were unlikely to master otherwise.

FINAL WORD: TO MAKE THIS CHANGE, WE MUST UNDERSTAND THE PHENOMENON OF CHANGE

Putting technology at the service of education means *change,* an aspect of life with which schools are uncomfortable. Misconceptions about technology, the role it can play in schools, and the impact it will have, stem largely from this resistance to change.

Underlying the lack of understanding is the need to force something new into a familiar mold, to impose structures of understanding that are traditional onto something that isn't.

Because the nature and degree of the change that technology will bring to education is profound, it is difficult for many to embrace.

There is serendipity here, though. In doing the hard work needed to create a fertile and receptive climate for the adoption of technology, we have an opportunity, perhaps even a need, to look at the phenomenon of change in education. Something not often reflected on in education is change itself and the relationship that educators have to it.

In order to make this change, we must understand the phenomenon of change. In the end, this must happen before we can move into the technology-supported learning space that is looming before us.

CHAPTER 4

Let There Be No Doubt

It is the supreme art of the teacher to awaken joy in creative expression and knowledge.

—Albert Einstein

Do not train children to learning by force and harshness, but direct them to it by what amuses their minds, so that you may be better able to discover with accuracy the peculiar bent of the genius of each.

—Plato

> What are some examples of programs that are easy to implement, adapt, and customize—that are instructionally rich and are supported by the use of technology?

WHAT DO YOU DO WITH THE TECHNOLOGY?

Once teachers are given access to technology, what comes next? Earlier in the evolution of instructional technology, answering this question was a serious dilemma. While the technology represented a set of powerful tools that impact the way people store, retrieve, and process information and communicate, it didn't provide teachers with concrete things to do.

A minority of teachers rose to the challenge and created activities to take advantage of the new resources. Or they invented ways of adapting the things they did before the technology arrived, making them more compelling, interesting, and relevant. But this was beyond the creative capabilities of the majority. It is also labor intensive, a disincentive to professionals who are largely overworked without having to blaze new trails.

This has since changed. There are now wonderful, good-to-go activities and resources available in abundance. Many of them are free. The technology itself has helped educators surmount this hurdle. Because of the miracle of the Internet, the idea of many sharing in the fruits of the labor of a small number of trailblazers has been realized. Under the aegis of a wide variety of organizations, content and resources have been created and placed in the virtual repository of the Web. The average teacher can tap these easily. The results are startling.

The following section will highlight a few of the valuable resources waiting to be put to use. There are far more available than can ever be used by any one teacher. It's a great pity that few educators are aware of this mother lode. It's all there: content, ready-to-use activities, and the stuff newbies can use to get their bearings and grow more confident in their use of technology.

By taking a close look at this growing body of easily replicable, budget-friendly resources, projects, and activities, we can get a glimpse of technology's potential to profoundly impact education. Here's a glimpse of the future of education.

The Peace Diaries Project: Education Transformed
www.peacediaries.org

How does technology transform education to fit our current world and the needs of twenty-first-century youngsters? How can it do this while satisfying the classic educational needs for learning basic skills? There are literally thousands of projects under way, designed and headed by educators, formally trained or otherwise, that anticipate the way education will work in the near future. Some of these projects attract attention while others simply give a group of young people the intellectual ride of their lives, without much hoopla. One sterling example of this shadow revolution is the Peace Diaries, a project that has engaged over 15,000 students in fifteen countries in a collaboration to trade ideas, research, and reflect about their cultures, and to write eloquently about them and publish.

The project's website (www.peacediaries.org) describes it as "an international education program developed by the not-for-profit organization Knowledge iTrust (KIT)." Students from countries around the globe utilize Internet technologies developed by KIT to learn, share, and collaborate on projects that produce educational content and global dialogue. This is disseminated through the Peace Diaries website, books, and radio broadcast.

In January 2002, Knowledge iTrust launched the Peace Diaries as a response to the September 11, 2001, events in New York City. *Peace Diaries* volume 1, a 300-page book on human rights and peace, was published in June 2002 with works from eight countries.

Karen Kaun, founder of the project, when interviewed for this book explained:

> On January 11, 2002, I was a guest speaker at Tech to Go, the New York City Public Schools Technology and Learning Conference. The room was packed and teachers and school administrators were standing in the hallway to listen to my overview of a new program I was introducing entitled the Peace Diaries. I explained that the Web-based Peace Diaries and its curriculum would help students in classrooms in New York City to learn about the lives and cultures of students from other countries. It was four months after September 11, 2001 [the World Trade Center tragedy], and teachers in New York City were seeking solace for their students.
>
> I am one of the most unlikely and most likely people to have founded an international peace program for children. I'm the most unlikely because I had no formal background in education and teaching until I began my graduate studies at Teachers College Columbia University (nearly a year after we launched the Peace Diaries program). I'm the most likely because I believe we humans can do anything when we put our undivided attention to. And practically speaking, my background in technology and my lifetime interest in other cultures, countries, and languages played a large role in the birth of the Peace Diaries.

The Peace Diaries would not have been possible without the extensive use of technology. Based on its exemplary achievement and the extensive experience it has accrued in bringing teachers to technology, we interviewed its creator at length for this book.

Mark: There is a significant amount of technology available to teachers. However, the rank and file are not embracing it to a great extent. What can you suggest to address this?

KK (Karen Kaun): It isn't enough to show teachers technologies that will make their lives easier. What they need to see are concrete examples of how to bring technology into instruction. For Peace Diaries, one of the keys to success is that we handed teachers a whole curriculum, soup to nuts, and said to them, "here's our technology—here's how to get it and use it in the classroom—here's the standards that it supports in English language arts and social studies." This is really important because teachers are really pressed for time and are preoccupied with helping their students pass high-stakes tests. There's hardly any leeway for trying new things or activities that don't relate to preparation for the tests.

Mark: A number of instructional technology leaders have come to the conclusion that the technology itself will not motivate teachers to use it, but projects that are laid out for them will get them onboard. Do you agree?

KK: Yes! We included teachers in planning the Peace Diaries, and we continued listening to them as we developed the program over the two and one-half years of its life. We took into consideration the things that they told us that they wanted to improve in their curriculum. We also took into consideration the way that they use Web-based technology and included that in our design. Everywhere I go I tell people that it is really important to have teachers decide these things. Corporations tell you that they have think tanks and ways of testing their products with teachers . . . but I just have this feeling that they don't do it one quarter as much as they should. If they did I think there would be far better designed technology for the classroom. I haven't seen very many products for use in classrooms that make sense from a usability standpoint. And of course, we've seen a lot of failure. These larger corporations that produce software are coming from a business environment. And business uses software very differently than teachers in a classroom with students do.

It's also true that children use technology very differently than adults do. My own children are growing up with technology as toys all around them. My daughter is so far advanced in using technology that it's ridiculous. She's taught herself how to program in Flash. No training, she just got a very basic introduction from a friend of mine who uses it. Afterward, she simply went off and created her own Flash animated cartoons.

Mark: That's a really interesting point. What would the implications be for a teacher who may not be that accomplished with technology but who has technologically adept students in her class?

KK: I took a hypermedia class at Columbia University last summer. I was doing HTML and a little bit of JAVA. I actually got help from my daughter, who's only eleven. She knew where to go on the Web to get access to a JAVA applet library. Well, she showed me how to use the applets to modify my website in ways I didn't know how to . . . it was great!

It's impressive learning from youngsters. I brought my project into my class at Columbia and the other students wanted to know how they could access the Java library as well. They wanted to do the kind of things my daughter had showed me. So there's an example of an eleven-year-old teaching adults who are interested in learning Web design. And one of the reasons that she knew all this is because she has time to go out on the Web and just play and look into tech communities that interest her. There are all these kid communities where they are actually building Web pages and sharing their work.

Mark: How did she find out how to do this?

KK: Kids just talk. It's word of mouth. When something is exciting they share it. It's like everything else with kids.

She jumped in the pool, learned a few strokes, gained some confidence, learned some from her friends, and learned some from the Web itself.

And then there she was, teaching herself and revising her own website based on the feedback she got from peers online. This is something I'm going to have to look at more closely as we build out projects through Peace Diaries, getting suggestions from students about how to do it. This type of thing was suggested by Papert and MIT. This is true constructivist teaching. You let the children take the ball and run with it. They construct their knowledge together and the teacher really is someone who is, I'll call her a mediator, somebody who participates in the construction of knowledge, but not somebody handing down knowledge. In the world of technology that's not a bad place to start from. There's so much to keep up with, I don't know how anyone, even a total geek, can stay on top of it all. But imagine thirty kids together. Each has her own bit of knowledge about technology. By putting together that brain trust to work collaboratively in a classroom, some extraordinary technology-based learning projects will result.

I keep coming across this thoroughly shopworn cliché about how technology changes the role of the teacher from the sage on the stage to the guide on the side . . . but really this falls short of the mark, because in this scenario the teacher is not the guide on the side; the teacher is a part of the core experience. The teacher is an active learner, the teacher is a partner, and she may be empowering the student to teach her. There is something very active and dynamic about this role.

Mark: And if we have adept youngsters in class, are we ready to have technology as an integral part of the instructional program?

KK: The way things are set up these days, with everyone concentrating on passing the tests, it almost seems impossible. I'm not talking about teachers who run a computer lab. That's one step removed. Technology use, obviously, is built into that situation. I'm not sure if we're going to see much technology use in a typical classroom today. We might have to start with real in-depth dependence on technology for instruction in an afterschool program. Then it might trickle down into the regular classroom, later on.

Mark: How do teachers' attitudes toward technology affect the course of your project? Do you have a self-selected group that is already over the hurdle of accepting technology? Or do you end up with teachers who are still flirting with the question about whether they can use technology or not?

KK: For the most part, their district selects the teachers who came into my project because they have some proficiency already. And, of course, the teachers we work from other countries have to have tech skills because there's no way I can get there to give them training. But the New York City teachers who found out about Peace Diaries from attending the Tech to Go conference were teachers who showed up on a Saturday with little more than an interest in trying. Because they were assured that this would be doable for them, they opted in. The theme of the project is what drew them in, in the first place. In NYC we didn't just throw curriculum at them and say "here you go!" We did professional development and then we were in the classroom working with them and their students. If they had questions, we were there, either by phone, by e-mail, or in person!

Mark: Did the assurance of support help get them over the "I'm not sure if I can do this" barrier?

KK: Yes! And inevitably there were technical glitches but they were patient with this. But that may be because Peace Diaries is a free project. And probably also because we sincerely tried to help them every step of the way. Support is always important. I hear about programs where things go into place and teachers are left to fend for themselves. When the project fails, unfortunately, sometimes the conclusion is that technology is not a viable resource for the classroom.

Mark: Do you see a shift in the attitudes of teachers about technology at the end of their involvement in Peace Diaries?

KK: Oh yeah! They don't need such a high level of support any longer. We've even had instances where teachers became our trainers. Not surprising. We made the tools pretty darn simple to use, so really, once you understand it, you log on and get to work. Students use the online tools on the Peace Diaries site to write their essays and to upload their artwork. We added another tool set this last time around, where a student could actually collect some scientific data that is related to what they are doing in the project, and we save that on our servers. The technology is like a pencil. It's just something that helps you get your work done.

Mark: So you went out of your way to design this as an easy-to-use set of applications?

KK: Right. We made them highly intuitive because, otherwise, the technology would have been a barrier instead of a facilitator. Technology was important to this project because it enabled us to bring together teachers and students from thirteen different countries. We created an online community of thinkers and writers on important subjects. It's important to note that the literacy aspects of this project, as well as the reflections on global issues, don't really require the use of technology. But the technology is what makes the project come alive.

We worked with a lot with a special education classes up in the Bronx on this project. Those kids often feel bad about themselves. But they were really excited to be using a laptop and contributing. Their work was published and they saw it on the Web. They were able to communicate with kids in other countries about things that they cared about and that was just amazing. One of the teachers is always asking me about when we are going to start another phase of the project. He tells me he loves this project because it makes his kids feel so special. (2004)

Involvement in a single project or experience can make a confirmed believer out of a teacher. The number of opportunities for further involvement are staggering and growing constantly as the following discussion suggests.

COMPUTER PROJECTS AND EXPERIENCES

Math-Kitecture: Can This Much Fun Really Be Educational?
www.math-kitecture.org

The Math-Kitecture project website asks the right question, "Can this much fun really be mathematical?" This website actually makes the experience of studying mathematics worthy of twenty-first-century kids. That's no small accomplishment. This free project utilizes technology now common to classrooms everywhere.

Math-Kitecture is the invention of Charles Bender, a teacher and instructional technology staff developer. The project's website (www .math-kitecture.org) provides all the explanatory text teachers, students, parents, or lifestyle learners need in order to understand the common math/architecture connections exploited through its inventive activities. Participants are encouraged to learn how to design functional living and working spaces and to create drawings that illustrate them. The site's text explains how to do this in detail. Its navigational plan is doubly instructive as it gives a great illustration of how hyperlink-driven text can provide each reader with a unique experience. The reader follows his own learning needs and instincts to find the right items in the right sequence. The result is the construction of a learning support as the learner constructs his own meaning. And this is just the beginning for Math-Kitecture participants.

Architectural plans created by project participants can be done with digital drawing programs or with conventional paper and materials. Afterward they are scanned and saved as common computer files. The files are sent as e-mail attachments to Bender, who uploads them to the Math-Kitecture website. There, they reside in the online student work gallery with the offerings of fellow Math-Kitects from around the world.

Math-Kitecture fosters learning in the areas of reading, mathematics, drafting and fine arts, and technology. Alexandra's rendering of Mrs. Doliber's classroom in the Terrill Middle School of Scotch Plains, New Jersey, or the work of Keisha, a seventh grader from Liberty Junior School in Liberty Township, Ohio, would seem to indicate that, yes, this much fun is very mathematical indeed.

IEARN: Not All Travelers Need Invent the Wheel
www.iearn.org

One of the tremendous advantages technology offers educators is that it eliminates the burden to continually start from scratch, a condition that comes from working in isolation. The Web makes it easy to inform oneself about wonderful wheels already in motion, vehicles that are good to go and to which one can hitch one's star. Few individual educators have the time, insight, creativity, and resources needed to put together an innovative curriculum-based project that will unite youngsters across great distances, and do so in activities that are motivating, satisfying, and rich in the stuff of great education. Fortunately, there are organizations that have made participating in such projects easy. Those not already in the know may be startled to learn that such opportunities are no longer rare. The menu of possibilities is dizzying. No group has done a better job than iEARN, an organization that many feel has set the standard for this new approach to education.

The iEARN website (www.iearn.org) states that "iEARN (International Education and Resource Network) is a non-profit organization made up of over 20,000 schools in 109 countries. iEARN empowers teachers and young people to work together online using the Internet and other new communications technologies. Approximately 750,000–1,000,000 students each day are engaged in collaborative project work worldwide." Since 1988, iEARN has pioneered online school linkages to enable students to engage in meaningful educational projects with peers in their countries and around the world.

iEARN describes itself as "an inclusive and culturally diverse community, a safe and structured environment in which young people can communicate, an opportunity to apply knowledge in service-learning projects, a community of educators and learners making a difference as part of the educational process."

"There are over 120 projects in iEARN, all designed and facilitated by teachers and students to fit their curriculum and classroom needs and schedules. To join, participants select an online project and look at how they can integrate it into their classroom."

"With the project selected, teachers and students enter online forum spaces to meet one another and get involved in ongoing projects with classrooms around the world that are working on the same project. These projects enable students to develop: research and critical thinking skills, experience with new technologies, cultural awareness, the habit of getting involved in community issues."

"In addition to connecting students' learning with local issues and meeting specific curriculum needs, every project proposed by teachers and students in iEARN has to answer the question, 'How will this project improve the quality of life on the planet?' This vision and purpose is the glue that holds iEARN together, enabling participants to become global citizens who make a difference by collaborating with their peers around the world."

ThinkQuest: Web-Based Content *by* Students *for* Students
www.thinkquest.org

The ThinkQuest competition is open to students around the world. This program promotes multicultural collaboration and learning by encouraging students to develop creative, informative websites. The competition runs semiannually with different topic categories.

Students between the ages of nine and nineteen are invited to form teams of three to six students, supervised by a teacher-coach. Teams choose a topic and produce a website to educate about it.

The projects are evaluated through a two-step process that includes peer review and scoring by professional educators who serve as volunteer judges. Sites that meet the evaluation criteria are published in the popular ThinkQuest Library, a free public resource of lessons created by students for students. Contest winners have received prizes from the program sponsors, including travel to the annual ThinkQuest Live event.

Teachnet: Teacher-to-Teacher Empowerment
www.teachnet.org

With the near ubiquity of new communication technologies, teachers have been empowered to reshape their profession as never before. The media, now democratized so that individuals anxious to be heard can publish their ideas with relative ease, makes it possible for concerned, inspired practitioners to spread their work and beliefs without the need for approval from an official authorizing agency. Thousands of teachers have published the fruits of their experience on the Web. A particularly well-orchestrated, illustrative example is Teachers Network.

Its website (www.teachnet.org) states,

> Teachers Network is a nationwide, non-profit education organization that identifies and connects innovative teachers exemplifying professionalism and creativity within public school systems. Over 40,000 public school teachers have received Teachers Network grants and fellowships in the areas of curriculum, leadership, policy, and new media.
>
> A professional community of teachers and educators working together to improve student achievement, Teachers Network serves 21 national and international affiliates that have adopted one or more of our major program initiatives.
>
> Knowing that teachers know best what teachers need, our goals are to support teachers in designing their own professional development, to document and disseminate the work of outstanding classroom teachers, and to help provide teachers with the knowledge and skills to become leaders in their classrooms and schools.
>
> TeachNet seeks to improve student learning by helping teachers develop appropriate and effective instructional materials that infuse the Internet and support local and state standards. Teachers have access to curriculum and technical specialists, grants, and a supportive network to further develop their skills throughout the year. Teacher projects are published online and disseminated to educators both locally and worldwide. These teachers are in the vanguard of educational reform, ensuring quality control of classroom instruction and responsible use of technology.

Among a rich selection of free resources, teachers will find numerous lesson plans for exciting technology-based projects, each of which has its own website replete with instructions and samples of student work. One interesting example is Postcards from Abroad (www.teachnetlab.org/is24/lvelez/postcard1.htm). The project's Web page states,

> Purpose of the Project: Postcards from Abroad empowers students to use their computers in a creative manner. First, students will learn how to search the World Wide Web efficiently, using Internet search engines and strategic commands. Then, they will learn how to edit digital photographs using HyperStudio software tools. Finally, they will create composites which will include a recognizable "background" from a faraway vacation

site, and a personal photograph. As a result, the culminating project will feature the creator and friends at a fantasy vacation site somewhere in the world, i.e. "virtual postcards."

ALI: The Fruit of Technology Experience
www.ali.apple.com

The Apple Learning Interchange (ALI) is one of Apple Computer's programs for education. It contains many free, ready-to-use items. ALI is offered to the world by means of its website (www.ali.apple.com).

The technology required to take advantage of ALI's resources for teachers and students is basic: computers and Internet access. Some also require the use of a digital camera (still or video), an item that can be rotated throughout a school and that costs far less than replacing a set of textbooks.

ALI projects sizzle with the excitement of learning in the new digital media age. Want to see examples of youngsters using twenty-first-century digital media to learn in ways they never could without it? There are numerous examples of such work here that was produced by typical classes. One is a middle school science item: Elements Commercials. Watch the videos produced by students in Lincoln, Illinois, to be entertained and learn. Teachers may want to replicate the project with their own students. Or they may want to use the project as a model in order to create a newer, farther-reaching project of their own.

The ALI site gives the following description of the project: "Most students are curious when they see a periodic table. Combine this curiosity with their love and knowledge of commercials and you have a powerful learning situation. Student teams create a presentation that will cause everyone in the class to remember the elements."

The site provides teachers with detailed instructions on planning, preparing, and implementing such projects with their classes. As an example, see the following excerpted snippets for the project mentioned above:

Outcomes: After completing this project, students will be able to: Understand metals, non-metals, metalloids, solids, liquids, and gases, identify important characteristics of all elements, and, interpret information about an element using the periodic table.

Technology Skills: After completing this project, students will be able to: Use AppleWorks to create a word-processing document, research a topic on the Internet. Use a digital camcorder to record presentations. And, use iMovie (free digital video editing software) to capture, edit, and share the commercial.

These projects are good examples of instruction that produces learning in both traditional content areas as well as in technology understanding.

Seeing is believing. Why not go to the site and click on the icons to launch some of the videos and review the work of middle schoolers Alex, Blake, Nathan, Chris, Robyn, Alexa, Kranti, or Priyanka. You'll learn about phosphorous and platinum and about how instruction can be empowered to engage youngsters for effective learning.

Scholastic.com: (Almost) Too Much of a Great Thing (http://scholastic.com)

Scholastic.com, the website of Scholastic publishing house, is such a vast trove of treasures for youngsters and those hoping to impact their education that attempting to describe it is almost futile. Technology-supported and enhanced activities abound in language arts, math, science, and social studies.

Of the dizzying array of offerings, perhaps the most compelling is a series of activities entitled Writing with Writers. There you'll find sections for biography, book review, descriptive writing, fairytales, folktales, and mystery writing. These online activities allow youngsters to get to know the writers of their favorite books in a way that is far more compelling than that offered by the average author website. Youngsters not only get a juicy biography about the author, including a digital video interview, but are tutored to become a writer in that author's genre.

To take this to its logical conclusion, students, on completing a piece, can upload it to the website and be published alongside their mentor. Further, in some cases the author may give the young author professional feedback on his efforts. In others, the author may invite students to join in a collaborative writing project.

United Streaming: A New Technology Saves an Older Cousin (www.unitedstreaming.com)

United Streaming is a yearly subscription service that is frequently paid for by departments of education or organizations that support education.

In New York State, for instance, PBS (Public Broadcasting Service) provides the service free of charge to all interested teachers. United Streaming provides a library of over 22,000 video clips that present core curriculum content.

The United Streaming website states that "*unitedstreaming* is a digital video-on-demand service brought to you by United Learning. Find out what 25,000 schools and over 10,500,000 students and teachers already know—*unitedstreaming* works!"

With unitedstreaming, you get

- The largest and most current K–12 video/video clip library available today
- The only standards-based video-on-demand application shown to increase student achievement
- Practical teacher and student learning resources
- Access to a wide variety of producers—United Learning, Discovery Channel School, Standard Deviants, Weston Woods, and many more
- Unparalleled options for customization and local control

The long lamented failure of television technology to revolutionize instruction may be reversed by the advent of the Internet's recent refinement, streaming video. Educators have long noted the value of educational content on television. Sesame Street, the Discovery Channel, and the Learning Channel are compelling and valuable, but when offered as broadcasts they fall short of impacting our education establishment because of the problem of coordinating instructional time with broadcast time. Video on demand allows the teacher to call up content at the moment it will add to the lesson.

NASA
www.nasa.gov/home/index.html

Here's a definite return on tax dollars invested in the space program: NASA's education website. This extensive collection of resources is a good example of Internet technology put into the service of learning. The site has numerous interfaces that the user can select, including ones created specifically for kids, students, and educators.

There are materials for teachers, for teachers to use with students, and for youngsters to learn with directly. A great deal of material is interactive with students selecting options and influencing outcomes as they navigate the site. There are animated simulations and videos in abundance as the site explores theme of astronomy, space travel, physics, meteorology, and related subjects.

Among other special features are Ask the Expert offerings in which students can e-mail astronauts and scientists to ask questions. There is also a great deal of technology-enhanced science news prepared for young people. There are games, cartoons, edutainment and information, and information.

Smithsonian Education: Museum without Walls
www.smithsonianeducation.org

In a sense this site is a vehicle by which the vast body of knowledge that is the Smithsonian Institution can be brought into classrooms everywhere. The museum's collection of artifacts is leveraged to produce the site's content for teachers and students. Consequently, primary documents valuable for education that would otherwise be hard to access are made available.

Various engines designed to assist teachers in searching through an extensive body of lesson plans are provided. In many cases there is a great deal more here than simple plans. The search engines turn up lesson packages that are replete with the content and resources needed to implement the lessons with students.

There is also a path through the site for students. The items accessed this way contain many interactive features and are intended for youngsters to use directly. The games and activities are entertaining, engaging, and educational.

World of Reading
http://worldreading.org/writereview.php

Here's one from the Ann Arbor District Library. It is free and requires no learning beyond the most rudimentary word processing and web surfing skills. For those who are afraid that technology discourages today's generation from appreciating books, here's an item that is doing just the opposite. Ann Arbor has established a vast portfolio of book reports written by youngsters for youngsters that are posted on its website. Prospective readers may search these by title, author, or location (city, state, school).

Nothing turns kids on more than talking to one another. World of Reading has harnessed technology to channel this natural facet of the behavior of youngsters to relevant learning activities. Furthermore, it takes an old, hackneyed item and breathes new life into it. Nothing is more classic to school than the book report. This bit of drudgery has been transformed into something exciting.

Motivation to write? It's all about having an audience. Knowing that kids from around the world will read your pearls of wisdom about what's worth reading definitely motivates. The tool to submit one's own book review is very simple to use.

MarcoPolo: Slam Dunk for Instructional Technology
www.marcopolo-education.org/index.aspx

MarcoPolo has been around for years and has undergone various evolutionary stages. It is an awesome collection of ideas and resources, all of which are free and easy to use. This enormous Web resource may well be the brand of instructional technology that will finally establish it as an essential resource for education.

MarcoPolo offers a comprehensive, one-stop-shopping approach to technology use for teachers. It is especially useful for those who don't necessarily want to become techies but want to take advantage of technology's offerings. This is a megasite with subsidiary spaces for literacy, math, science, humanities, economics, and the arts. Each discipline's website in and of itself is an extraordinarily deep and rich resource.

MarcoPolo offers lesson plans, activities, and the content to support them. It also offers online tools, interactive software that gives the learner the capability to travel further and deeper in following challenges or self-directed inquiry. A good deal of the very best in teaching practices is embedded in these tools. Teachers would be hard-pressed to research, acquire, and organize a set of resources like the one found free on MarcoPolo.

Furthermore, the experience that can be had by learners here, particularly when mediated by a savvy teacher, will rival any a teacher could provide. The site's resources, by the way, are aligned to state learning standards. They will resonate loudly with teachers who are looking for something beyond the traditional text but must continue to function within standards-grounded schooling. It is traditional enough to reassure the raised eyebrows of administrators and school boards.

The brief description at the top of the MarcoPolo home page states, "Marcopolo: Internet Content for the Classroom. [MarcoPolo] provides the highest quality standards-based Internet content and professional development to K–12 teachers and students throughout the United States."

Here's a brief overview of the MarcoPolo site's components:

ReadWriteThink (www.readwritethink.org) is a state-of-the-art literacy resource that was developed in collaboration with the International Reading Association and the National Council of Teachers of English. The approaches and practices to teaching and learning literacy skills represent the best thinking and experience in the field. The twist is that the site offers software, a rich portfolio of interactive tools that expand the learner's capability far beyond that to be found in a paper-driven classroom. The tools set offers a wide variety of graphic organizers and visualization pieces. These support essential understandings in reading and understanding literature. The tools also represent real advantages in the publishing of student work, an essential step in the process of writing.

Illuminations (http://illuminations.nctm.org/index.html) was created in collaboration with the National Council of Teachers of Mathematics. The site offers many dozens of activities, interactive software tools, video clips, inquiries, and investigations. All of these coalesce to form a vast body of practice and support that help establish a new and revitalized mathematics education for today's youngsters.

The tools, which at this writing number approximately forty, include an electronic abacus applet, the fractal tool, the graph creator, an isometric drawing tool, a sound sketch tool, a tube viewer simulation, and a shape pan balance. There are virtual manipulatives, simulations, spreadsheets, and software engines.

Science NetLinks (www.sciencenetlinks.com) is the science component of MarcoPolo. "Providing a wealth of resources for K–12 science educators, Science NetLinks is your guide to meaningful standards-based Internet experiences for students."

The site contains lessons and activities and has reviewed and linked them to some of the best Web-based resources produced by science education organizations from around the world. Accordingly, the variety of visually rich, animated, and sound-enabled, highly interactive items to support Science NetLinks content makes it one of the best resources ever developed. Students will love the videos and game-style actions. Educators will easily recognize how easy this resource is to integrate into what they are already doing when they read statements such as: "To help educators integrate Science NetLinks resources into a standards-based curriculum, all site content is organized around the Benchmarks for Science Literacy. These benchmarks are a set of science literacy goals developed through Project 2061, AAAS's long-term initiative to reform K–12 science education."

EDSitement (http://edsitement.neh.gov) is the humanities component of MarcoPolo and offers a wealth of lessons and activities organized around four basic categories: art and culture, literature and language arts, foreign language, and history and social studies. These can be searched by theme and grade level.

The lessons are supported by hyperlinks to relevant, exciting resources culled from the World Wide Web. For instance, a virtual tour of a cave in the south of France displays the wall art of early man. Content and links to support the entire context required to understand this amazing phenomenon are included. Another site is devoted to the culture of Native Americans. There, among an assortment of video-style, game-based learning activities, one can weave one's own unique wampum bead belt. To study the relationship of man to animal as a classic form of myth, one is whisked to a site on vanishing and extinct creatures and encouraged to learn about them. This is made concrete by the need to choose one to portray in the creation of a virtual postcard. The card can actually be e-mailed to a friend. This site truly makes humanities come alive.

EconEdLink (www.econedlink.org) is devoted to teaching and learning about economics. Like other portions of MarcoPolo, this one offers a library of carefully crafted lessons and activities that are supported by a broad selection of interactive, information-rich resources purveyed by the websites of organizations worldwide devoted to explaining economics.

The final piece of the continuum of social studies is geography, and this is served by the National Geographic Web component entitled Xpeditions. Xpeditions offers hundreds of pages of content on the world and its peoples, creatures, and places specially crafted by National Geographic for youngsters. In addition to the lessons and activities, standard features of a MarcoPolo affiliate, there are special software tools to support the understanding of geography. These include such items as customizable, interactive digital maps, Xpedition Hall, the site's virtual museum, "where every click brings geography to life," and a Homework Help area, where students can "find pictures, articles, facts, maps, and more on top subjects—perfect for reports!"

The final component of MarcoPolo is *ArtsEdge* (http://artsedge .kennedy-center.org), which was developed under a cooperative agreement between the John F. Kennedy Center for the Performing Arts and the National Endowment for the Arts, with additional support from the U.S. Department of Education. In addition to providing lessons and activities that are aligned to and supported by rich, Web-based resources, the site provides a database-style engine that allows one to search for appropriate items by core curriculum content areas: ESL, foreign language, mathematics, science, or social studies. Or the search can be done by arts areas: design arts, language arts, performing arts, or visual arts. This enables those interested in engaging in arts activities to easily accomplish something that traditionally is difficult—aligning the various arts to traditional subject area learning. ArtsEdge has also published the best lesson plans of arts educators from throughout the nation, enabling other teachers to benefit from their work and experience. The site actively solicits additional submissions.

FINAL WORD: MUCH MORE TO COME!

In the time it has taken to write and publish this book, undoubtedly a great deal more of the type of material highlighted in this chapter has been added to the burgeoning accumulation on the Web. Fortunately, the technology itself presents the solution to the problem it creates by offering such a massive overabundance of opportunities and choices. The proliferation of metasites in which Web-linked resources are aggregated for specific audiences and purposes and increasingly varied and user-specific search engines will keep the information glut manageable for educators. Those who spend a little time informing themselves about how to locate and navigate these resources will be greatly rewarded.

See chapter 6, "The Convergence of Education and Industry," for additional resources and details.

CHAPTER 5

Saying Nay to the Naysayers

The principal goal of education is to create men who are capable of doing new things, not simply of repeating what other generations have done—men who are creative, inventive and discoverers

—Jean Piaget

Keep away from people who try to belittle your ambitions. Small people always do that, but the really great make you feel that you, too, can become great.

—Mark Twain

> Can any breakthrough escape defenders of the status quo? Can negative rhetoric provide positive direction for the instructional technology revolution?

MISINFORMED, MISGUIDED, AND PREVENTING AN IMPORTANT CHANGE

By now the arguments against the adoption of technology for education compose an extensive body of discourse. These ideas have been popularized and legitimized by a group of self-styled experts who have grabbed a good deal of attention for themselves by promoting them. There are some out there who argue against a role for technology in education for altruistic reasons. Although these folks may be well intentioned, they are misinformed and misguided, and ultimately they contribute to preventing an important change from taking root.

While many of the arguments make sense, at least on the surface, in general they are based on a lack of understanding about what technology can do for education and what the likely impact of its broad-based adoption will be. Buried within this mass of muddled thinking are some insightful, legitimate concepts that will actually enrich our understanding of the place of technology in teaching and learning.

One upside down, chicken-or-egg argument points to the modest amount of technology that has been purchased and deployed in our schools and accusingly declares it a wasteful, damaging mistake. The technology that is there, it claims, simply isn't used enough to justify its having been purchased.

As unfair as this position is, its logical extension is far worse. Follow this argument and eventually it calls for the removal of the technology already in place, freeing up "valuable" space, time, and focus. And then, of course, it would be folly to buy any more technology from that point on.

BUMPS IN THE ROAD TO TECHNOLOGY ADOPTION

Imagine a biblical fiscal watchdog taking Noah to task for spending so much on lumber. Clearly, there was no need for such a massive ship with so little water around, right? Or, to use another analogy, the accepted wisdom during the 1930s and early 1940s was that Congress was wise to skimp on developing and maintaining our armed forces. After all, why waste precious funds on defense when there was no threat to be seen anywhere? And of course, up through December 6, 1941, this made a great deal of sense.

If computers have touched intellectual activity in every aspect of human existence, then why not education? In every field in which technology has been embraced, there was a transition period replete with bumps in the road. There was a time, for instance, when many in banking considered the use of ATMs a screwball notion with very little chance of success. That this was a shortsighted understanding of a new application of computing is an extreme understatement. ATMs have drastically improved banking in our world and perhaps represent the most far-reaching innovation in that industry in a century.

Education is currently experiencing such bumps in the road to technology adoption. It has stumbled and tripped over potholes as it has inelegantly taken its first few baby steps. Attempting to get up to speed on the road to the appropriate and wise adoption of technology has been marked by mistakes and small failures. Harping on these may generate book sales and public speaking fees for a few, but it has also fueled and given respectable justification for something else—a significant sentiment among the greater educational community that can only be described as a committed backlash against the use of technology in our classrooms.

Some of this backlash can be ascribed to pure reluctance to change. Many teachers and their supervisors feel threatened by such a profound change or, at the least, disquieted and uncomfortable. As this book has pointed out time and again, underlying this is a lack of understanding about how the technology can support and enhance education.

The perceived threat also stems in large part from a series of misunderstandings about how adopting technology for education represents a wrong turn, a distraction, a digression, and even a direct threat to what they feel are the true goals of education.

Fueling and furthering this wrong-headed backlash are a handful of popular books written by self-proclaimed thought leaders on the subject. Numerous articles and several reports have tried to table or marginalize the agenda of technology as a vital, integral part of the twenty-first-century educational landscape. Let's take a look at some of the prominent objections.

THROWING THE BOOK AT INSTRUCTIONAL TECHNOLOGY

Some notable titles are *High Tech Heretic,* by Clifford Stoll (1999); *Failure to Connect,* by Jane Healy (1998); *Oversold and Underused,* by Larry Cuban (2001); and *The Flickering Mind,* by Todd Oppenheimer (2003).

Few of the thousands upon thousands of schools in the United States have not attempted to use some level of technology for instruction. To truly understand this initiative would involve extensive research. Typically, and understandably, this hasn't been done by most who have written on the subject.

Larry Cuban, in his book *Oversold and Underused*, relates his observations and conclusions in visiting a small number of schools, mostly in

Silicon Valley, the epicenter of technology sophistication. Cuban observed that while technology was present in the schools and classrooms he visited, it was largely unused, or perhaps used for noninstructional purposes.

Taken at face value, it might appear that he is presenting a simple and obvious truth, that if something is purchased in the hope that it will make a difference, and then turns out to be hardly ever used, the purchase was made inappropriately and the mistake should not be repeated. However, it should be kept in mind that we are not talking here about purchases of average items, like desks and chairs. Rather, the subject of his argument is the stuff of a far-reaching revolution in the way humans function as intellectual creatures. Missteps are part of the overall change process and it is unreasonable to assume that humans would get something of this complexity and gravity right in their first attempts.

Cuban is quite correct in asserting that aggressive sales forces have taken advantage of well-intentioned but gullible school boards in selling more computers early on than could possibly have been used appropriately. And now, in a sense, they have killed the goose that laid the golden egg because technology purchases are not viewed as part of an exciting experiment, but as if they were textbooks, something that is already established and from which demonstrable results should reasonably be expected.

In his book, Cuban asks many important questions about why we are technologizing our schools, what we hope to get out of doing so, and what results we are actually achieving. Unfortunately, particularly in respect to the latter, it doesn't appear that he's done a particularly good job in seeking answers.

Most of the schools in which Cuban did his observations are located in Silicon Valley. At first glance this might seem an advantageous place to conduct such research. After all, who should know more about using technology, be more receptive to its adoption, be more willing to engage in revolutionary experimentation, than the residents of the center of technology innovation and the educators who serve them? But is this a good argument? Does it logically follow that because a community derives a good portion of its prosperity from producing technology it automatically knows how to tap that resource in groundbreaking ways to educate students?

Both well-heeled communities (like those in the valley) and challenged inner-city neighborhoods need revolution in the way they approach education. Consequently they can make good use of technology,
if they truly understand the advantages it offers. Perhaps the two types
of school environments would use technology somewhat differently,
but both ought to take advantage of this remarkable, as yet largely un-
tapped set of resources. Seeking out and citing examples of effective
technology use would help schools determine how to employ it best.
Instead we are primarily given examples of wasteful or counterproductive technology use.

FUEL FOR MISGUIDED FIRES

Other books draw similar conclusions. One recent addition to this
genre is Todd Oppenheimer, *The Flickering Mind,* which some feel attempts to invalidate the entire field of instructional technology.

In his review of the book, Bob Blaisdell from the *Christian Science
Monitor* states, "What impact has computer technology had on public
education in the U.S.? That's the question journalist Todd Oppenheimer
sets out to answer in *The Flickering Mind.* Mr. Oppenheimer's conclusion: Putting computers in classrooms has been almost entirely wasteful,
and the rush to keep schools up-to-date with the latest technology has
been largely pointless" (2003).

These are powerful statements and in the hands of folks like typical
school board members, who generally do not have instructional expertise; they can be fuel for many misguided fires. Those interested in identifying places to make budget cuts could easily construe such statements
as a godsend. The consequences for the quality of the instructional program offered youngsters in schools without technology as it finally finds
an appropriate groove, however, may be felt for a very long time after
the current budget and educational philosophy crisis have passed.

The *Monitor* states, "Of course, this is not the first time U.S. schools
have been seduced by new technology, Oppenheimer points out. He
summarizes the history of technological innovations in American
schools and explains how each (TV among them) has been hailed as education's savior" (2003).

How ironic that this particular concept, practically an icon of failure to comprehend the nature and power of technology to enhance education, should be trotted out. Yes, a good deal of rhetoric was tossed about in the early days of television about a possible transformative impact on education. But no significant funds were ever expended to make this so, at least not directly in schools.

PBS and the Discovery Channel clearly demonstrate that television can marry with education to produce something wonderful. But broadcast TV never made much of a splash in public schools. The logistical problems involved in accessing this programming were simply too severe. However, since the advent of the VCR, it would be hard to find a school in the United States in which instructional videos have not become a standard feature of the educational program offered to contemporary youngsters (who see video as a baseline item for any environment they function comfortably in).

Those who are paying attention to the way content is purveyed on the Web and the way that content is prepared and packaged for education know that finally, more than fifty years after the beginning of commercial television, streaming video technology is making the use of video practical in our classrooms. It is not the case that the lack of television use proves that technology cannot be tapped to improve education, but rather that the new digital technologies finally offer a practical way to make this happen!

In the December 2003 edition of his online journal *From Now On*, author and classroom technology advocate Jamie McKenzie reviews Oppenheimer's book in an article entitled "One Flew Over the High School." To prepare himself for the review, he visited the schools that Oppenheimer mentions in his book. About Oppenheimer's book, McKenzie states, "His thesis is patronizing and poorly substantiated. . . . His book is fatally weakened by a focus on the negative. . . . He did not look very hard for good technology use. It is easy to find and quite abundant. . . . This is a strange book—a disturbing book freighted with bias and distortion."

Reading McKenzie's article, one might conclude that the anecdotes related in *The Flickering Mind* are not accurate or responsible and perhaps belie an author's motivation to grab some limelight while ignoring the impact that biased reporting produces. McKenzie relates in detail how his own visits to classrooms reveal the opposite of what Oppenheimer reports. He explains this in detail and convincingly justifies his position.

> The missing section . . . the book should have and could have told the stories of teachers who have made smart use of the new technologies and kept them in their proper place. While Oppenheimer maintains that such teachers are rare, merely accidental and mostly just anomalies, perhaps he was so endeared to his thesis and his preconceptions that he flew over such teachers and schools as he sought confirmation of his 1997 claims in *The Computer Delusion*, his article in *Atlantic Monthly* that first advanced his thesis.

REESTABLISHING LEARNING AS PART OF YOUNGSTERS' LIVES

Napa Valley High School, the focus of Oppenheimer's book, is a successful school situated in a well-heeled suburban community. With or without technology, education in Napa Valley will succeed. It would be far more interesting to see the impact of technology on inner-city schools in which success has perennially eluded teachers and students. The power of technology may include the ability to take schools that are functional and make them more so, a worthy goal; but its greatest worth will be displayed in its ability to reestablish learning as part of the lives of disaffected youngsters in our inner cities. Many have dropped out, literally or figuratively, by turning off to what is set before them at school.

SHALLOW PROPHETS AND DEEP PROFITS

Perhaps a backlash against technology for education is to be expected in light of the degree to which unrealistic claims surrounding it have established a climate of disbelief in its potential.

In his startling book, *School's Out: Hyperlearning, the New Technology, and the End of Education,* Lewis Perelman (1992) states,

> For a technological revolution is sweeping through the U.S., and world economies that is totally transforming the social role of learning and

teaching. This learning revolution already has made the "classroom teacher" as obsolete as the blacksmith shop. In its aftermath, most of what now passes for education "reform" will appear as useful to economic security in the 1990s as the Maginot Line was to military security in the 1940s. (p. 20)

He further states, "Nations that stop trying to 'reform' their education and training institutions and choose instead to totally replace them with a brand-new, high-tech learning system will be the world's economic powerhouses through the twenty-first century" (p. 20).

Such futuristic gee whiz dreaming is inspiring, heady stuff that does little to promote instructional technology as the stuff of practicality. Schools will never be eliminated, and the assertion that technology will eliminate the need for school is way off the mark. Schools do not exist solely for educational purposes but largely function as custodial institutions; something our society has great need for.

In their zeal to cash in on the sales potential of instructional technology, purveyors of equipment and software have made claims that have done significant harm. Undeliverable promises have disappointed buyers and their supporters and have cast doubt and disbelief on the entire field. Not all of this mischief can be attributed to a profit motive; lack of clear understanding about what it is that technology can and shouldn't be expected do is at the root of this problem.

As technology burgeons throughout society, the world of education will also be affected by it. Any new field that attempts to present itself often does not put its best foot forward at first. With profits uncertain, instructional technology entered the education market seeking some quick attention and wins, and often without extensive research and development funding behind the initial products and services offered.

PAINTING INSTRUCTIONAL TECHNOLOGY WITH A BROAD BRUSH

Early on, a good deal of technology was directed at "drill and kill" devices and software. The powerful processing and recall functions of computers were adapted to present youngsters with endless short-answer prompts to help them memorize facts more easily. This appealed to developers because it was an obvious way to produce a product based on technology. Unfortunately, there has been a guilt-by-association factor here. Educators have lost enthusiasm for any interaction between student and teacher that places high value on the recollection of facts and have consequently painted all instructional technology with a broad brush, assuming that this is what it is all about.

Even this simplistic approach is not without value. While a deeper level of fluency is the stated goal of education, memorization will always be a foundation for higher thinking skills. Seen in this light, programs that support memorization can free valuable teacher and class time from these chores, which can be performed at other times and other settings.

HYPE AND HYPERBOLE

William Rukeyser, affiliated with the organization Learning in the Real World and a spokesman on the subject of technology and education, is emblematic of those who have allowed suspicion of the sales ambitions of the technology industry to eclipse the good that technology can do. In a PBS interview (Rukeyser, 2000) he stated,

> If you take a look at the entire history of the twentieth century in schools, what you can see is this pendulum swing back and forth with someone coming along and saying, "you buy this gizmo," and it may be Bill Gates with Windows, or maybe Tom Edison with the black-and-white silent movies, but in any case, the innovator says, "Buy this and it will make schools obsolete, teachers irrelevant, it will bring the world into the classroom, if we even need a classroom, and it will make learning fun and easy, and almost effortless."
>
> The pendulum begins to swing with the sales pitch, and then you get the first results showing that it's not quite working the way the pitchman said it would. And then you get disappointment and then at the end, you get finger pointing . . . The innovator saying, "well, it's not working the way the innovator said it would." And then you get the gizmo going back into the box, and the last step in the pendulum swinging is kind of group amnesia. People tend to forget that it happened, and you are set up for the next swing of the pendulum, the next person coming in saying, "Hey, salvation is only a few billion dollars away."

Rukeyser is correct: technology has been hyped and the sales tactics of some purveyors have been aggressive and based in hyperbole. But the reasonable question to be asking is, can the hype be forgiven now so that we may seriously investigate how education can benefit from a truly extraordinary set of resources?

But technology is much more than the acquisition of things, their costs to buyers, and profits to sellers. In the same interview Kristi Rennebohm Franz, a teacher at Sunnyside Elementary School in Pullman, Washington, stated,

> We found software programs that helped children with keyboarding, helped them edit and publish their writing, and helped them email their writing. The software unencumbered the children's writing from using just paper and pencil, which is hard for their fine motor skills. So, you take the technology itself and how it can unencumber the writing/communication process and you put, on top of that, another layer of the social context in purpose and content of writing through telecommunications so children are writing to peers about what they know well . . . You put that known content together with having an audience of peers and a purpose for interactive communication and a piece of technology tool that unencumbers the process to communicate, and you've got a dynamite process for literacy!

THE E-PARENTING FALLACY

Another unfortunate misstep in identifying and presenting a place for technology in education has been the overhyping of e-mail and other telecommunications technologies. These have been proffered as the solution to the societal disconnect of parent involvement. Little holds higher ranking in the minds of educators than getting parents involved in the schooling of their children. It is the erosion of this involvement, many believe, that explains teachers' inability to control the behavior of youngster and engage them in school activities.

However, false prophets of technology claim that this problem can be solved by making communications easier and more practical. E-mail has indeed transformed person-to-person communications in general, but it hasn't altered the interactions between parent and teacher significantly. The issue in parent involvement does not stem from logistics in facilitating communication but rather in the motivation to be in touch. Parents for the most part are simply not interested in frequent, ongoing, discourse on their child's day-to-day school activities. Rather, they want to be reassured that all is well as the school takes care of their youngsters.

Similarly, in the ongoing battle to get youngsters to do daily homework, some tech wags have claimed that, more homework will get done when teachers post it on a website. Parents will be able to know what the assignment is, as well as when and how it is to be done and turned in. This may be. More likely, though, problems with homework stem from the motivations of teachers in assigning it, of students in doing it, and of parents in supervising it.

HERESY AND HEARSAY

Cliff Stoll is an astronomer who writes about technology. He is not a professional K–12 educator, and perhaps this is why the assumptions that underlie his ideas in *High Tech Heretic* seem so far off the mark. Consequently his book presents flawed arguments.

The book's subtitle, *Why Computers Don't Belong in the Classroom and Other Reflections by a Computer Contrarian,* speaks to the orientation of this tract. Like many professional contrarians, Stoll found an audience eager to watch him spar with an annoying bit of evolving conventional wisdom: computers are important. In a style reminiscent of Andy Rooney, he apparently explores and exploits that gray area between "Flat Earth Society" tilting at institutional windmills for the sport of it and serious reporting on an evil that has grown in the shadow of one of society's blind spots. Perhaps he feels that he has engaged in the kind of thing that Ralph Nader did in his book *Unsafe at Any Speed,* responsible arguing armed with real facts and figures. In this case, the supporting evidence, however, just doesn't appear to be there.

It would be easy to infer from Stoll's narrative that as a student he discovered how to discipline himself to work hard in school. Now, in reflective hindsight, he's happy that he took the obvious path to success in school and life: diligence. But, well-intended observer of schooling that he may be, he hasn't logged the requisite tens of thousands of hours working with a typical cross-section of today's youth that would afford him true understanding. He doesn't get it. Just because adults agree that youngsters should be diligent, disciplined, and motivated to study and learn doesn't mean that they will be. Like so many wannabe educators, he apparently can't see that understanding the value of those things and the reality of actually trying to bring them about are two widely separate realities.

TURNING LEARNING INTO FUN IS BAD?

For instance, he drones on and on about how uncomprehending instructional technology advocates mistakenly push for making learning fun. "Turning learning into fun denigrates the most important thing we can do in life: to learn and to teach. It cheapens both the process and product: Dedicated teachers try to entertain, students expect to learn without working, and scholarship becomes a computer game. When in doubt, turn to the electronic mind-crunch" (pp. 13–14). He is very far off in his assessment. Making learning fun and entertaining does not necessarily dumb it down or lessen its value. On the contrary, it makes learning accessible to a vast multitude of youngsters for whom it would not be, otherwise. When he talks about "the most important thing we can do (learning)" is he mindful of the actual percentage rates of learning that our population is now evidencing? Does he understand that traditional methods continue to produce failing results? When he states, "Most learning isn't fun. Learning takes work" (p. 12). what pool of expertise is he tapping into?

One example of the inappropriate use of technology (in his opinion) that he gives is software entitled NFL Math. "The program forces the child to do a math problem in order to be rewarded with two minutes of entertainment. Then the torture begins anew. What a great way to teach hatred of math" (p. 17).

Has Stoll recently looked at any of the traditional 400-page, 7-pound, 80-dollar math textbooks that are sold by the millions to schools determined to provide mathematics instruction to youngsters? Many would consider them a far better way to teach hatred of math than the software Stoll denigrates.

What these naysaying theorists don't understand about the motivating, entertaining aspects of what technology has to offer education, is that in order to be engaging, a lesson need not be a video game, hip-hop video, or sitcom. It needs to be relevant! Stated another way, it needs to be a good learning opportunity, one that youngsters can see the point of, enjoy laboring at, and feel a sense of accomplishment and personal growth through their participation. This approach to education is not about providing a wonderful sugar coating for the bad-tasting medicine that students reflexively avoid because it is painful or unpleasant to them. Nothing could be further from the truth.

COMPUTER LITERACY *AND* LITERACY

Stoll's book is chock full of articulate but half-baked opinions. For instance, when he asks, "Which do we need more: computer literacy or literacy?" (p. 9). he falls into the classic *either/or* trap. No, Cliff, it's not computer literacy *or* literacy; it is increased literacy learning through the focused, responsible use of technology, implemented by an adept teacher!

Need proof? Go to the ReadWriteThink website (www.readwrithink.org), a free resource produced by a partnership of the International Reading Association, the National Council of Teachers of English, and the MarcoPolo Education Foundation. Chock full of standards-based lessons, activities, and resources, it is a good example of what you'll actually find if you really look to see how technology use can support and enhance literacy learning.

Interestingly, Stoll makes good sense when he asserts that computer literacy is not a worthwhile pursuit for most students to invest much time in during their academic careers. He hammers the point home by stating,

> When I point out the dubious value of computers in schools, I hear the point "Look, computers are everywhere, so we have to bring them into the classroom."
>
>   Well automobiles are everywhere too. They play a damned important part in our society and it's hard to get a job if you can't drive. Cars

amount for more in our economy than do computers: General Motors' revenues are many times those of Microsoft. But we don't teach automobile literacy. Nor do we make driver's education a central part of the curriculum . . . (p. 9)

When taking his shots at the computer's impact on mathematics learning in the chapter "Calculating against Calculators," Stoll seems to trip himself up by not thinking out the logical extensions of his attacks. He deplores that math software goes straight to answers without calling for or honoring the reasoning process behind it, and attacks the use of calculators because they perform arithmetic calculations, delivering instant results. But in doing so, they free youngsters to concentrate on higher order processing and problem solving—helping, not hurting, learning to reason. Furthermore, it is absolutely not true that math software doesn't call for thinking, processing, and, at times, defending the evolution of one's answers. There are numerous programs that do that. And if drilling youngsters to memorize basic facts like times tables is of value, as Stoll states, then an entertaining, nonjudgmental, endlessly patient entity like a computer game is precisely the vehicle through which this can be achieved.

What Stoll appears to call for in this book is the mediation of technology carried content by a teacher. Yet he continually falls into the hole of seeing computers as being used solely in the mode of individual students confronting software on their own. "After all, the computer is a one-kid-at-a-time experience," he says. This common misconception comes from observing how some educators, motivated by the practical, logistical considerations of shoehorning computers into the old, established structure of school, and with no long-term body of practice on which to draw, may have mistakenly implemented a technology program. There are many other ways of deploying computers in our schools. Students need not use them in one-on-one isolation.

NAY IS JUST THE FLIP SIDE OF YEA

While laying down arguments against the use of digital technology in educating our young, the naysayers have actually established a good vantage point from which the overwhelming value of instructional technology can be seen.

The vision of education that the naysayers collectively purvey is an archconservative one. In their opinion the new technologies and the new possibilities for education that they bring represent impediments to the effective reinvigoration of the failing traditional ways that schools have been operating for over a century. To listen closely to their philosophy is to hear the conviction that our nineteenth-century form of public schooling is appropriate but neglected. If we would just renew our commitment to it, if we would simply marshal our forces to make it work again, everything would be fine. In their view technology is a blind alley, a digression, an expenditure of precious funds and time that pulls us away from the obvious (to them) benefits of traditional, print-based schooling. But their arguments against the use of technology are based in large part on observations, assumptions, and conclusions that are not true.

Technology represents far more than powerful resources waiting to be tapped. To understand how technology has changed our ways of data collection, research, analysis, synthesis, and the communication of facts, ideas, and discoveries; to understand how it has altered the storing and retrieving of information; to comprehend how it has altered the ways that humans work together and share resources, is to understand a radically changed world. In this new world aspects of traditional schooling have become outmoded. In some cases this is because the technology has rendered it so, but in others it is because traditional ways of functioning were already cumbersome that technology was developed to offer an improvement.

Of the two groups that stand firmly in the way of the adoption of technology for education—those who just don't get it and allow it to lie fallow and those who actively stand against it—the naysayers may be the more benign. They keep the conversation going, get the arguments on the table, and pave the way for progress once their considerations are quelled. Naysayers enliven the discussion and move bystanders to reflect and take a position.

Unfortunately, books are often used more as bludgeons for the defense and advancement of partisan agendas than as food for thought and reference for the honest and serious quest for the truth. Jane Healy's book is often cited by those questioning the adoption of computers in the classroom. The book's title, *Failure to Connect* (1998), suggests a negative stance toward instructional technology. This, however, is not the case.

TECHNOLOGY SHAPES THE GROWING MIND

The book is better described by its subtitle *How Computers Affect Our Children's Minds for Better and Worse*. Healy opens the book by saying, "Technology shapes the growing mind. The younger the mind, the more malleable it is. The younger the technology, the more unproven it is. We enthusiastically expose our youngsters to new digital teachers and playmates, but we also express concern about the development of their brains, bodies, and spirits. Shouldn't we consider carefully the potential and irrevocable effects of this new electronic interface with childhood?" (p. 17).

This is a noble premise on which to base a book and the research behind it. However, she seems to be saying that before we deviate from the unquestionably functional and healthy environment that is represented by the classic version of public school, we should make certain that the alternative is better. But is that a good description of the educational experience afforded most youngsters currently? Not likely. Much of what we offer our youngsters is so far off the mark that there isn't much to risk and probably a great deal to gain. Furthermore, a lot besides technology that is unproved in its effect on young minds is continually introduced into our schools. They actually function as laboratories, at least in the area of teaching and learning.

Healy is right on the money when she states, "Without adequate planning and sound educational rationale, computers will be either misused or unused. Teachers are overwhelmed and resistant" (p. 66). Unfortunately, our experience points less to computers being misused than unused; or perhaps misuse comes first, leading to dissatisfaction and disentanglement, and then come reluctance and evasion of using them.

Perhaps, when she wrote the book several years back, the idea expressed in the title of her book's first chapter "Blundering into the Future: Hype and Hope" was true. No longer. There is enough experience behind us so that our efforts need not be blundering. The hype of the past hasn't poisoned the well so thoroughly that we need turn our backs on technology just as its responsible, effective implementation becomes doable.

FAMILIAR PATTERNS OF OLD PARADIGM THINKING

In her first chapter, Healy debunks the assumption that youngsters need to know how to use computers. She interviews Harvard professors who concede that their students need to use computers but could learn to do so in a short period of time and would be better off knowing how to read, communicate, and think. But isn't this a familiar pattern of old paradigm thinking? Couldn't it be that in learning to read and communicate, technology plays a valuable supportive role? Or perhaps this was more legitimate an issue when the book was written a while back, when free Web resources like ReadWriteThink, Scholastic.com, and Reading World weren't so ubiquitously available to all on the Web.

Another section she titles "Challenging Change," as if that were possible. Technology-driven change is not something to be challenged. It is here already. We can accept it or deny it. But either way, it has altered the world irrevocably. We can't go back.

Healy continues throughout the book seemingly making the assumption that the ways she sees computers being used for instruction are the only ways they can be used or will be used. Not so. While it may have been true for the teachers she spoke to, that they were largely unsure of how to use technology, a great deal of it now has been crafted to build on what teachers do ordinarily without computers. There need be no head scratching about how to use technology in class if an honest, intelligent effort is expended to understand this.

In her chapter "Computing Basics for School and Home" she states,

> The computer revolution in education involves far more than simply finding new ways to help kids learn. It challenges some of our most deeply held beliefs about how children should be raised and educated. Much of the abysmal state of today's educational technology results from failure to confront three basic issues: 1) technology's potential to alter the adult-child balance of power and change schooling as we have known it; 2) the implications of software choices; 3) appropriate planning for computer use at home and school. (p. 37)

The second and third items may seem obvious but certainly are valid. Concerning the first, let's simply ask, Do we feel that the teacher-centered, autocratic style of the traditional classroom is something we are satisfied with and have decided to keep?

Healy quotes an anonymous media executive from a Connecticut suburb as saying, "I want my son to learn history, not spend his time at school playing computer games!" But does she bother to show this parent websites like the Smithsonian's, where his son can examine primary documents more effectively than he could at school?

Healy is certainly right when she cites as very poor teaching practice putting children at computers to direct their own efforts at using demeaning, simplistic software that offers them the opportunity to play silly games as rewards for getting a few multiple choice questions answers right. But instructional software has moved beyond that, far beyond. Furthermore, the solution to these dismaying situations is not to eliminate technology from the educational experience we provide but to involve ourselves more deeply and demand that a rigorous, challenging, and worthwhile one is provided.

QUALITY SOFTWARE IS OUT THERE

Perhaps the poor quality of much of what Healy experienced in schools using computers has much to do with educators telling themselves that the technology program wasn't worth the time and effort they invest in other areas and consequently was neglected? It is heartening that she gives tips on choosing software. But in doing so she demonstrates that quality software is, in fact, out there and if this is the case, why spend so much time showing examples of schools that don't take advantage of it? The kind of irresponsible teaching going on in the computer rooms she points to also goes on in math, language arts, science, anywhere that the time and effort needed to ensure that instructional time is well spent hasn't been taken and children are left to fend for themselves.

Lamentably, a quarter of the way into the book, Healy offers extended advice to those who run schools about the strenuous efforts required to make a technology program work, which must be very discouraging to many who read it. Technology need not be such hard work; if approached properly, it can lighten things up rather than bog them down.

Unfortunately, Healy is right on the money in concluding that "the most striking thing so far is the magnitude of the 'gee whiz' factor—'wow look what the computers can do' compared with the lack of discussion about good reasons to do it" (p. 79). There was a good degree of truth to this when she wrote the book. Happily this has largely changed and continues to do so.

DEVELOPING INTELLECTUAL AND PERSONAL WORTH

Healy asks great questions, for example, "Do I risk being stoned in the public marketplace if I suggest that the purpose of education is not to make kids economically valuable, but rather to enable them to develop intellectual and personal worth as well as practical skills?" (p. 106). The question is right but the significance is skewed. Doesn't today's technology, the resources available on the Web for instance, promote the things she's concerned about?

Healy asks the expected question about the effect that staring at screens and hunching over keyboards will have on young eyes and bodies—without asking the more important question: Is sitting at a computer work station the way that youngsters should use computers? Or would another approach, say, a single computer projected onto a screen for group discussion, work better?

She interestingly asks what the effect of using artificial intelligence to educate youngsters will be. But in the end, the artificial intelligence of computers is created by the natural intelligence of people and is thus shaped to reflect our needs and satisfy them. True, we may be educating our youngsters to develop their minds differently than predigital generations did, but there is nothing to be done about this other than to do so carefully. The die is cast. Today's young will grow up to enter a tech-dominated world. End of story.

LOOKING FOR GOLD IN A DIAMOND MINE

Healy is not alone in her concern about the mix of technology and youngsters. There is another publication that purports to sound the alarm bell concerning the dangers of computer use for children. Several years back a widely publicized report entitled *Fool's Gold* was released by the organization Alliance for Childhood. The report, however, seemingly conforms to the shallow, prejudiced thinking embodied by much of technology naysaying. Interestingly, it poses many concerns that are similar to those voiced in *Failure to Connect.* The report's executive summary states, "Computers pose serious health hazards to children. The risks include repetitive stress injuries, eyestrain, obesity, social isolation, emotional, or intellectual developmental damage" (p. 3).

Clearly, these are widely held concerns. But, again, only a literal transposition of the approach to working with computers that is experienced by corporate workers in their Dilbert cubes to the elementary school classroom would have the framers of the report make such assumptions. Youngsters need not benefit from technology by having them work isolated at a computer. Duh!

The report goes on to say, "Childhood is a critical phase of life and must be protected to be fully experienced. It should not be hurried" (p. 1). But how does a teacher hurry childhood by presenting language concepts to the class by launching Riverdeep software's singing noun frog and letting the various students decide how quickly to advance the program?

The report further states, "Children also need time for active, physical play; hands-on lessons of all kinds, especially in the arts; and direct experience of the natural world. Research shows these are not frills but are essential for healthy child development. Yet many schools have cut already minimal offerings in these areas to shift time and money to expensive, unproven technology. The emphasis on technology is diverting us from the urgent social and educational needs of low-income children" (p. 3). Truly, if that is the case, then the report is performing a valuable public service in pointing this out. There is nothing about the value of technology that ought to eclipse other, vital needs of developing youngsters. Robbing Peter to pay Paul can never represent a responsible approach to education.

FINAL WORD: WILL NAYSAYERS HOLD TOMORROW AT BAY OR HELP US EMBRACE IT?

In her book, Healy (1998) gives a list of suggestions on how to ensure that computer use is developmentally appropriate. Of course, in doing so, in effect, she concedes that this is eminently possible. Why, then, didn't she focus more on this rather than catalog the many possible ways that computers might throw a monkey wrench into the work of developing young minds?

The final section of her book relates precepts about how and when technology may be used and used well in educating the young. In including this material she both makes the case for technology and begins some of the work in laying groundwork for that to happen. Quite possibly, given the opportunity to ventilate and a sympathetic listening ear, the naysayers will purge their negative energies and become advocates for the appropriate use of technology in our schools and learning environments.

CHAPTER 6

The Convergence of Industry and Education: A New Relationship for a New Education

Education's purpose is to replace an empty mind with an open one.

— Malcolm Forbes

I want to put a ding in the universe.

— Steve Jobs

In transforming yesterday's classrooms into today's digital learning environments, is business friend or foe? What came first, the computer for sale or the instructional need for it?

A RELATIONSHIP RECONSIDERED

In the past, educators took a "don't you dare come into my house" attitude toward the business sector. The advent of technology and the sweeping changes it brings, though, have forced a reconsideration and, in many cases, a change in this attitude. As a result, the relationship between business and education, and ultimately the type of education provided for twenty-first-century youth, is changing profoundly.

Where schools succeed in bringing technology into the instructional program, industry plays an increasingly important role. Even schools that have resisted technology find themselves targeted by salespeople as never before.

One might think that the technology agenda would have trouble picking up momentum as a result of confusion about the kinds, quantities, and deployment models of technology for instruction, the consternation about where to get the funds to acquire it, and the endless head scratching about how to get teachers to use it. However, there has been a take-it-on-faith element in the equation that represents a very powerful force. Although many people aren't quite sure why technology should be in schools, they feel that schools must have it. This ultimately detracts from the true value of technology in our classrooms.

AN UNDENIABLE, UNSTOPPABLE
FORCE HAS MADE ITS WAY INSIDE

Parents, school boards, and the general public see the prominence and power of technology throughout our society and want young people to have this as part of their education. This push has given the technology industry a kind of moral high ground from which to lobby for an unquestioned place at the table. Many in charge of school budgets, even those who mistakenly see no educational value in technology, have not dared to oppose its purchase. Getting technology into schools has become an unquestioned and unreflected-on goal. Parents who scarcely can afford a computer at home or understand why their child must have one fall in line and buy one. Nonprofits like the Scouts and others that serve youth reflexively include technology in their programs. And it truly makes sense to want the greatest innovation in intellectual work to constitute part of the landscape, wherever the mission is to positively impact the intellectual growth of our young.

Whether the reasons motivating technology acquisition are the right ones or not, the instructional technology industry is a constant presence, an undeniable, unstoppable, smiling force that has made its way inside the palace of education. Those who historically were kept at arm's length are now welcomed in. This is an unanticipated and, to many, a disarming change.

This situation merits reflection. Whether one approves of the trend or not, the seductive power of this marketplace cannot be avoided. Schools must shop, compare, acquire, and deal with business as never before. And businesspeople must learn the ways of education and become part of it in order to achieve their goals. At the end of the day, sales goals and purchasing budgets aside, there remains the possibility that industry, school, and private citizens involved in education can take advantage of the dynamics of this rich marketplace to further the agenda of education.

STUFF FOR SALE

Schools, educators, parents, and students have always interacted with business out of necessity. The ten thousand and one things that schools must acquire, everything from books to pencils to toilet paper, is purchased from vendors. Also, preparing youngsters for the world of work, to take their place in the world of business, has often been cited as the prime purpose and goal of schooling. Although there is a long history behind the relationship between school and business, the roles have always been clear and the boundaries well defined. Furthermore the relative importance and value of the things offered for sale in the past was easy to comprehend. Clearly, much has changed.

The instructional technology industry—computers, software, and related items for education—has promoted a vision of a just-around-the-corner educational tomorrow in which technology is the defining force. This vision features a new type of school and classroom, an educational environment in which there is a deep saturation of technology items. Obviously, it is in the economic interest of the industry to promote this vision. Doing so is tantamount to creating and growing a market for its wares.

Unfortunately, the education sector is ill equipped to respond. Some simply reject the vision, holding on to an outmoded paradigm and depriving twenty-first-century learners of an appropriate instructional environment. Others accept it without defining for themselves what and how much is needed and how it will be used.

Doing a Web search using "education" and the name of any of the major computer manufacturers as key words, the result would be a variety of websites that sell computers. One states that the company "provides any combination of desktop and notebook computer lab configurations, as well as computing solutions for the school, campus, and district administrative office. . . . education customers can choose from networking solutions including wired and wireless, as well as highly competitive prices on our full line of servers, desktops, monitors, notebooks and accessories" (an anonymous computer manufacturer). Needless to say, computer manufacturers are very interested in selling computers and have targeted schools as a marketplace. This is not surprising.

THE HOLY GRAIL OF INSTRUCTIONAL TECHNOLOGY

One outgrowth of this campaign is the mythical holy grail of instructional technology, the one-student-to-one-computer ratio. If we believe that youngsters should use computers, then schools should have a computer dedicated to each youngster's use. Much has been written and said about this arbitrary gold standard of computer deployment in schools. But is it based on educational reality? On real needs?

While corporate office culture often establishes a one-to-one ratio between employees and computers, there are other models of professional people using technology where this is not the case. Hospitals, for instance, do not provide a computer for every nurse. One or two terminals per nursing station seem to be adequate. Likewise, it is not a foregone conclusion that schools must model themselves after corporate headquarters and provide a separate terminal for each student or a similar implementation mode that features a high saturation of technology items. Perhaps there are better ways to bring technology into the intellectual lives of our young people. The same is true for connectivity, networking, software and online content, and so on.

Real instructional needs should be used as the best measure of how much technology to acquire and how to deploy it. A one-to-one ratio may be appropriate in some settings for some purposes. One to thirty may be adequate in others. Some learning activities may require powerful computers with rich content software; others may be done off-line with simple word processing or other tool software.

A NEW, DEEPER RELATIONSHIP BETWEEN THE TWO WORLDS

Acquisition tied to real needs does not necessarily short-circuit the sales aspirations of Silicon Valley. The outcome can be a high level of computer purchases overall, as purchases satisfy the needs established by instructional activities. Sales goals should not dictate instructional programs, something that has happened as educators are pressed to put equipment to use in order to justify its purchase. Satisfying the needs of students and teachers can satisfy the tech companies as well. What's needed is a new and deeper relationship between the two worlds.

Even so, schools should consider acquiring some technology with room-to-spare advanced capability. Experimentation with powerful machines often opens up possibilities that spark creativity and offer unimagined opportunities for teaching and learning.

Many instances of success in transforming a school's instructional platform into one that features technology have been accomplished because industry is part of the picture and part of the conversation. Not as an outsider but as a partner. This is a significant change. Schools and home learners have traditionally gotten by with simple, low-cost resources: a stack of textbooks, a ream of paper, even a copy machine or two. With the advent of technology for education, this changed very rapidly. Resources are no longer simple or inexpensive. New companies out to grab their share of a new market have targeted schools as a prime source of sales. Schools, ordinarily cool toward the prospect of purchasing, have been in a hurry to catch up with the information age and are susceptible to the sales pitches directed at them.

The term "partner" is used in the business–school relationship as never before. School systems going from no tech to tech intensive have had to make high-stakes purchases. They have had to throw their lot in with one vendor or another to take advantage of broad-based software deployment that literally redefines much of what they do. The school's partner and his solution can influence the style, nature, and success of what is done in the school. What can emerge from the purchase and relationship are ways to get more technology in use, more quickly, more cheaply, and more effectively for the tasks of education. While business sees that education represents a substantial market, much more important than it was understood to be previously, schools must rely more heavily on the business sector in order to get their mission accomplished.

FREE LUNCH

While much of the products and services for sale are offered in a straightforward manner, pretty much in the same context as buying pencils and toilet paper, something new and different has emerged, something far more interesting and significant than simply what is for sale. This market has redefined the idea of free lunch.

Nobel Prize–winning economist Milton Friedman's oft repeated statement "there's no free lunch!" no longer bears the same significance in the technology age, when free lunch abounds. Free e-mail from Yahoo! and Hot Mail, free digital storage from Web services, endless examples of "freeware" and "shareware" software to be downloaded and used, and free content, services, and tools of every conceivable kind are to be had online. In the digital age there is free lunch aplenty! Like a hungry man bewildered by access to an endless buffet, teachers may find the choices and volume overwhelming.

Some of the freebies are available because companies understand that getting people used to using technology by giving them free-to-use items is a good way to develop a market. A new user who starts out on free software will return to buy other software. Some of the wealth amounts to free samples: "Please try our basic software, perfectly adequate to get the job done, by the way, and hopefully you'll trade up by purchasing our deluxe version later on. Or perhaps, you'll just tell your friends about it and they'll be the ones to buy."

Digital content, once it has been developed and made available on the Web, costs the provider little more for a thousand users to download than it does for three. The increased cost factors are almost negligible. There is as much inducement to produce and upload it as there is to download and use it. When a corporation produces a booklet suitable for use with students as a PDF file, schools everywhere can download and use it with little cost to the producer, something that never could be true with books.

THE DUAL NATURE OF CONTENT

Companies have caught on to the dual nature of content. It can function as content for the consumer and advertising or public relations material for the business that produces it.

Two related market dynamics that often come into play in this type of scenario are mind share and advertising. One of the great truisms about the Internet is that the old saying, If you build it, they will come! is definitely not true. A company may craft a wonderful advertisement in the form of website, but an audience will not necessarily materialize to view it—unless you give that audience a good reason to go there.

For that reason, there are websites by the tens of thousands that offer wonderful, advertising-free content. But the user must drift past advertising to get to it. Online newspapers are a good example of this. A print copy of the *New York Times,* at this writing, costs a dollar, but the online version is free. The news items are essentially the same as those in the print version. Of course, one is subjected to advertising to get to this online news, but that is also true of the print version, which requires the reader to shell out a dollar.

Some websites sell advertising space. Some are run by companies that use the traffic that the site's content draws as an opportunity for retailing. On the Internet, this "mind share" is a valuable commodity that drives commerce.

Parent and child advocate groups often voice strong objections to subjecting youngsters to the commercialism of the Internet. Newspapers in Education, the formalized, institutionalized use of traditional newspapers as an instructional resource, is an acceptable, desirable instructional practice. These programs bring large numbers of print newspapers into classrooms. It is ironic, therefore, that the same sort of advertising that one finds on the Web is found in those newspapers. Wise educators might take advantage of what is offered and even turn it into an opportunity to have youngsters reflectively, critically form life strategies about how to deal with the commercialism that exists all around them.

FREE RESOURCES FOR EDUCATORS

An encouraging aspect of our new technology-dominated intellectual environment is the free resources that industry has made available to educators though the Web. This is true for all sorts of companies; everything from power utilities to retailers have loaded the Web with an inconceivable amount of content that is useful in the education of our young people, much of it created expressly for that purpose. Taken with the online materials provided by our cultural institutions, non-profit organizations, and universities, the Web represents the greatest library ever assembled or imagined by man.

Major players in the technology industry—Apple, IBM, Intel, Microsoft, and others—have developed and made available online, rich resources for educators that provide lesson and activity plans, practitioner reflections on how to use them, and technology in general as a resource for teaching and learning. They are comprehensive, providing students, teachers, parents, and others the materials they need.

The education section of the Microsoft website is a good example. In addition to a link on the How To Buy page, there are links for tutorials, lesson plans, templates, clip art, and faculty development, all of them representing free items similar to things that have been purchased with real dollars at other times, in other contexts.

And there are middle-ground items as well. The same page offers administrators a No Child Left Behind Funding Opportunities link. Helping schools find dollars they may have overlooked is good business for companies that are anxious to relieve them of such funds in exchange for goods and services.

The free resources provided by the tech industry represents a unique opportunity for educators who would be wise to familiarize themselves with it. Unfortunately, the offerings are so copious, varied, and spread out across the Internet that becoming aware of what is out there and how it can be used is no mean feat. The list of online goodies is extensive, as the following section suggests.

Technology Hardware Producers

Offered Online by Intel

The Intel Corporation manufactures chips and processors that power most of the world's personal computers and has long offered free resources to educators.

Learning Projects: Discover Great Teaching Ideas (www.intel.com/education/sections/section1/index.htm). This Intel site features an Innovation Odyssey page brimming with technology-rich project ideas for teachers of every subject, teaching style, and grade level. It shows how teachers around the world use technology in exciting ways to support student learning—from navigating the Idaho outdoors to inventing toys in Israel. A different story is featured for every day of the school year. The site also provides an in-depth showcase of the planning, implementation, and assessment of a technology-enhanced roller-coaster design project.

Innovation in Education (www97.intel.com/scripts-seeingreason/index.asp). Among the many gems offered on Intel's Innovation in Education free Web resource is Seeing Reason, an online mapping tool. *Seeing Reason* is a classroom workspace for investigating cause and effect relationships in complex systems. At the heart of Seeing Reason is an interactive mapping tool that helps students map relationships and construct models of their understanding.

Seeing Reason offers a complete resource collection. If this is your first visit start with the Overview and Benefits sections that explain the whys, hows, and significance of the tool and the things that can be done with it. Try the Tool allows you and your students to practice building maps. Instructional Strategies shares recommendations from teachers who have used the tool. Project Examples, from teachers in different grades and subjects, will get you started with ideas and details for your classroom. A detailed chart illustrates the benefits of "making thinking visible" for your students. When you're ready to use the Seeing Reason mapping tool with your class, visit the Teacher Workspace to set up a project that will save individual student maps. Among a myriad of opportunities, one can visit the Site Recommendations page for technical specifications that optimize use of the Seeing Reason mapping tool.

The website includes a wonderful example of this kind of twenty-first-century learning activity in which socially minded sixth graders take on tough questions, such as, "Why are our roads unsafe" and "How can we make the world a safer place?" They think through the complex problem of road accidents with the help of the Seeing Reason mapping tool.

Offered Online by IBM

TryScience. Just read and browse your way through dozens and dozens of rich, entertaining science experiences. Occasionally, you'll left click your mouse to select and activate an icon. That's all the technology training you'll need to enjoy TryScience, a collection of museum and other science websites from around the world.

The TryScience website (www.tryscience.org/) "is your gateway to experience the excitement of contemporary science and technology through on and offline interactivity with science and technology centers worldwide. Science is exciting, and it's for everyone! That's why TryScience and over 400 science centers worldwide invite you to investigate, discover, and try science yourself. . . . a partnership between IBM Corporation, the New York Hall of Science (NYHOS), the Association of Science-Technology Centers (ASTC), and science centers worldwide."

The site's interactive activities include thematic interactive experiences, virtual field trips to science centers around the world, student polls and surveys, online science news links, and live views from Web cams at science and technology centers worldwide.

Offered Online by Apple

Apple computers have always been very popular in the education sector, which has been one of its principal markets. Apple offers free resources online that appeal to students, teachers, and others.

ALI. The Apple Learning Interchange (ALI) is Apple Computer's free program for education. It is offered to the world by means of the ALI website (http://ali.apple.com/). The site provides a wide variety of easy-to-use resources for educators. The technology required is basic—computers and Internet access. Some require the use of a digital camera, still or video, an item that can be rotated throughout a school and that certainly costs far less than a single set of textbooks. ALI is a powerhouse of resources provided by Apple Computer. The site has the standard features that one would expect of such an enterprise: lesson plans, student work samples, teacher reflections on instructional practice, subject content, and more. This is all done with Apple's particular focus—digital media publishing for teachers and students.

Understanding on a theoretical level that the production of media items such as student-created movies can bring spark and relevance to teaching and learning is one thing. Seeing in detail exactly how to do it in a classroom is quite another. The ALI site provides the plans, reflections, and samples needed to make it all clear.

One example is the Core Democratic Values LIVE project, "a cross-grade level activity between senior government and fifth grade social studies students. Teams create desktop movies depicting the concept of each one of the core democratic values and the relationship of that value to their own lives." The site provides numerous sample videos that were produced for the project. Supporting materials for this project (and numerous others) include items (many of them videos) in the areas of standards, assessment, reflections, step guides, technology, research, and background.

Another intriguing dimension of the ALI site is the virtual field trip section. Video lessons in areas such as science, culture, or history and with a particular focus on place, are cataloged and made available through links. The videos generally originate from museums or cultural institutions that have produced them as part of their own education program. The upshot of this is that ALI has aggregated and highlighted fine examples of video content for instruction. The effect is to provide a library of useful content, as well as a demonstration site for the potential and efficacy of digital video-on-demand to support teaching and learning. All of this is free for the using.

Good examples include Where the River Meets the Sea, an ecological exploration created by the Smithsonian and Ball State Teachers College; Race Rocks, an environmental virtual field trip produced by Garry Fletcher of Lester B. Pearson College; and Exploration of the Physical Science of Baseball, also from Ball State Teachers College.

The ALI site can be an invaluable resource for teachers new to the use of technology, as well as those who are seeking to take their tech-supported practice to another level. One item that can support this is the Technology Showcase section. Here, educators can get ideas for technology items that are designed to be within their grasp, yet take teaching and learning to new dimensions.

ALI is heavily laden with resources and is updated periodically. It cries out to be explored by educators who will undoubtedly figure out their best ways of learning from it and using its resources.

Computer Operating System Producers

Offered Online by Microsoft

The Microsoft Corporation produces the Windows operating system, as well as the Microsoft Office suite of software applications. This ubiquitous business software includes Word and PowerPoint, which are widely used in the world of education.

Microsoft Education: Virtual Classroom Tours (www.microsoft .com/education/default.asp?ID=InTeachersVCT). This is a rich collection of educational resources created by teachers for fellow teachers. As the site explains, "Teachers learn best from other teachers. Virtual Classroom Tours offer the resources to lead students through creative, constructivist, technology-rich projects for all grade levels and subject areas." The tours are downloadable PowerPoint files with project background and planning information, teacher and student reflections, content-rich teaching resources, and assessment and standards information. Submitted by accomplished educators from throughout the United States, the tours offer instructionally sophisticated insights into lessons, projects, and activities.

Internet Service Providers

Offered Online by AOL

AOL, the giant Internet service/online service provider, provides e-mail and communication opportunities to millions of people in the United States and around the world. AOL is home base for information and online communities of people interested in exploring common interests across the Internet. All of this for a fee. Many teachers are AOL members who communicate with one another through their AOL accounts.

AOL@SCHOOL (www.aolatschool.com). This comprehensive, Web-based resource site offers freebies such as content software and lesson plans, but its particular contribution is in the format in which its components are presented. AOL@SCHOOL, unlike free resources produced by other industry players, is presented in a portal format sim-

ilar to that of the Microsoft Internet Explorer home page, or of news organizations like CNN or BBC online versions.

Much of the material on this portal is not produced directly by AOL
but is culled and aggregated from other sources of free materials. The
material is presented and organized in a way calculated to appeal to educators, students, and parents and help them with their educational
needs. Most importantly, it is easy to use. The news portal format gives
the user a sense that the site is constantly updated. New items are presented constantly, which makes the experience of visiting this portal a
fresh one every day. Wonderful resources are archived and can be visited or located time and again.

Offered Online by CableVision

CableVision is a cable TV company in the northeastern United
States. Like other cable companies, it has entered the broadband ISP
market and has become a service provider to those involved in education. Cable Vision produces Power to Learn.

Power to Learn (www.powertolearn.com). A portfolio of online educational materials for students, teachers, and parents. This resource is
updated periodically and features a great deal of content that is produced specifically for this site. Notable components include an Ask the
Expert area in which students can meet an accomplished professional
in such areas as the arts, sports, social studies, and science. A different
expert is featured on an ongoing basis. Past experts have included
Spike Lee, Walt Frazier, and Marc Anthony.

There is also a School to Career section, as well as a host of instructional games. There are lessons and activities. Needless to say,
some of the resources showcase the advantages of broadband connections. For instance, there is a connection to a Web cam placed in
an osprey nest that gives a real-time look at goings-on in the nest, as
well as action-packed archived videos culled from the ongoing
recordings of the Web cam. In one segment, the resident raptor repels
an invader. There are also sections that show teachers how to use a
variety of technology as instructional resources and a section for
youngsters that illustrates how they can effectively use technology as
a resource for learning.

Instructional Software Producers

Offered Online by Riverdeep

Riverdeep (www.riverdeep.net) is a major producer of instructional software. Its Destination Reading and Destination Math titles, for instance, provide nearly complete courses in core curriculum areas. The software uses computer technology to create an entertaining, informative, interactive, and highly motivational educational experience for youngsters.

Riverdeep has put a free portfolio of highly useful, well-thought-out materials for educators and students on its website. The site performs several functions. On one level it is an online showroom for Riverdeep to display its wares for sale. As a way to accomplish this there are free resources and activities based on Riverdeep software products. Frugal teachers, parents, or students can find a great deal to do and learn without making a purchase. It is easy to see, too, how getting hooked on these materials could easily lead to purchases. The site establishes a good model for exchange of value between software producer and consumer. In an ideal world, the consumer will be familiar with software in general and prospective purchases in particular, which this site makes possible.

Offerings are wide and include such items as Baily's Book House Letter Machine ("Join friendly critters to learn letter names and sounds! Pre K–2"), Mighty Math Astro Algebra Calculator ("this unique calculator shows its work as you use it to help solve algebra problems Grades 7–9"), and Space Academy GX-1 Orbital Guide ("come explore gravity, trajectory . . . everything you need to know to launch into orbit").

The site also has a news portal. Article offerings are available in their entirety for the price of a mouse click and appear to be crafted by subject, format, and language level for youngsters. Unlike common news items though, they are thoroughly embedded with teaching and learning items, tips, and opportunities for activity extensions. The articles, when replaced with others in the portal frame, are archived and can be searched easily. One good example is "Along the Food Chain," a science article that discusses human impact on the environment through food harvesting practices.

Xcursion Central (www.excursioncentral.com). Perhaps the gem of Riverdeep's many free online offerings is its Xcursion Central. This resource's website poses the question, "You have computers in the classroom. Now what?" And further, "Educators realize the enormous potential of computers, but how do we effectively weave technology into the daily work of the classroom? How do teachers find the time to learn and prepare, to make sense of the dizzying array of resources available on the Internet? And how do we achieve core standards in education using technology—not for its own sake, but as a tool to enhance classroom lessons?" The resource modestly promises to be "one innovative and easy solution."

Xcursion Central offers Internet field trips, instructional experiences that are ready for classroom implementation. They are designed to be a safe way for students to access the rich content on the Web without the teacher having to do preparatory work.

The activities contain live websites that have been annotated to guide student thinking. These are created by teachers for teachers. They are classified by subject, theme, and grade level, containing learning objectives, activities, and opportunities for assessment. The activities enable students to safely and easily access content on the Web and use the information they gather to deepen their understanding of a wide variety of subjects. Additionally, they teach to multiple intelligences, encourage inquiry and active learning, support a variety of learning styles, teach students how to find, gather, organize, and assess information, lend breadth and depth to existing curriculum.

Offered Online by EduWeb

EduWeb (www.eduweb.com/index2.htmlis). Here are some marvelous online activities for youngsters. EduWeb creates activities for a variety of institutions such as museums and cultural centers. EduWeb doesn't sell materials to consumers but rather charges institutions for their creation. The website, in a sense, functions as an online portfolio.

In offering its services to prospective new clients, EduWeb highlights examples of what it has already created, making them available to all who care to use them. The quality of this free content is truly startling.

Gorgeously illustrated and animated, the site's offerings are highly interactive and engaging.

A good example is The Mystery of Apo Island, in which youngsters must hunt for virtual clues to solve a mystery that involves understanding nature, environments, ecosystems, and the scientific method. At the conclusion of the activity the students must present their solution to an ecologist who weighs the value of their hypothesis and gives feedback and encouragement. The piece is reminiscent of Tom Snyder Productions' Rainforest Researchers software, a popular item purchased by thousands of schools across the country. Apo Island is free for the taking and consequently a good example of how the Internet has changed things.

BrainPop (www.brainpop.com) is a popular subscription service for teachers and students. This type of service has become a common way for companies to market and for schools and individuals to purchase instructional software. Instead of acquiring content that is delivered on a disc or otherwise embedded in the hard drive of the user's computer, the customer goes to a password protected website, logs in, and gets access to the content. There are many advantages to both parties in such an arrangement.

BrainPop delivers content in a motivating, entertaining, and engaging manner by producing short animated videos on a wide variety of topics commonly taught in schools. The 300 or so titles (as of this writing) fall into the categories of health, science, technology, math, English, and social studies. The videos cover such themes as reading a newspaper, adding and subtracting fractions, and ecosystems. The videos follow the format of a conversation between an animated adolescent and his robot sidekick. As of this writing, BrainPop allows nonpaying visitors to access up to two videos per visit to their site. This is a good example of the free sample style of resource commonly available on the World Wide Web.

Print Publishers

Offered Online by Scholastic

Scholastic (www.scholastic.com) is one the most successful publishers and vendors of books and related materials for the world of education. In recent years it has embraced the Web as an extension of its print-based world. The Scholastic website offers a rich body of educational resources that are free for the taking and using.

Interestingly, while this company produces and sells software, including that of Tom Snyder Productions, an industry pioneer and standard setter, the Scholastic.com website has established a wonderful rationale for print publishers to offer free online resources. Educators are struggling with the thorny problem of what role The Book will have in our new digital age. Scholastic's site has done much to create a comfortable context for all to experience and resolve this. Consequently, the site's resources are very appealing and potentially valuable for the vast majority of teachers.

The site is organized into three sections by which the content is organized and accessed. One for teachers, one for kids, and one for families, which bears the motto "Encourage the love of learning at home." Scholastic's site is clearly intended to promote the sale of its books, periodicals, recordings, and other educational materials, but it accomplishes this in a wonderful way.

The site establishes a unique environment for young readers. The characters that populate Scholastic's wares are all here: Clifford the Big Red Dog, Harry Potter, the Magic School Bus, and so on. In the new world established by the presence of a variety of related media, these characters appear in books, move on to periodicals, and then to their own TV shows or movies. Or they make their rounds of various formats in a different order. The effect of this is an apparently seamless continuum, and the site is replete with free software activities that extend the lives and reach of the characters and themes, making for a literacy experience that keeps growing richer.

Entering the site's mountain of content through the kids' entrance, one is confronted with choices of games and engaging activities. Some, like Captain Underpants, are just for fun and replicate tried-and-true video/computer game formats, although populated this time with characters that are familiar to student readers. Other items (and there are plenty, like the Card Factory) have youngsters using visually and intellectually stimulating interactive software to read, write, evaluate, and produce products to be printed or e-mailed. This site is full of free items that involve youngsters in using their imagination and their literacy skills to do something in the real world. Many involve kids making decisions, taking polls, analyzing things, and writing reviews and critiques . . . good education.

This site puts youngsters in touch with writers as part of Scholastic's efforts to make writing come alive. The Book Central section is replete with profiles of writers, opportunities to be in touch with them, and ask them questions. No more tired old book reports scrawled on lined three-hole paper to be read to one's bored classmates. Scholastic offers the opportunity for kids to write a professional-looking review and have it published on the site for the whole world to see.

The offerings for teachers are equally exciting. The lesson plans and downloadable, reproducible work and instruction sheets are there, plus teaching tips and tools, free professional journals, the news portal with age- and grade-appropriate content and related activities, and more. The resources stretch out in an endless horizon but there is one of particular note. Teachers can easily craft their own class websites through the Scholastic site, which acts as host. It's easy, no Web authoring software, no FTPing updates. Simply use the teacher website tool like any other online form and have an instant website. Scholastic, the book publisher, makes teaching in the digital age easy, exciting, and free.

FINAL WORD: JUST THE TIP

The resources described above represent a piece of the tip of the iceberg, a small sampling of the free gems out there on the Web. What is food for thought, though, is that while so much is available, it is hard to find an educator who is aware of what's there, how to find his way to the right stuff, and how to use it. In essence, a treasure trove for educators is going unnoticed and unused. What is needed is a metasite, a home-base clearinghouse where all of the wonderful free resources on the Web can be listed, sorted, reviewed, and recommended. This growing Mount Everest of content and resources needs to be made accessible to the current cohort of teachers in our schools and others beyond, who are constantly searching for great materials to fuel their efforts in education.

CHAPTER 7

Higher Education: The Typewriter Generation and the Information Age

There is nothing more difficult to take in hand, more perilous to conduct than to take a lead in the introduction of a new order of things—because the innovation has for enemies all those who have done well under the old conditions and lukewarm defenders in those who may do well under the new.

—Machiavelli

> Higher education is a prime entry point and an important influence on how technology is perceived and used by prospective educators. What is the reality of the status of technology in course preparation and delivery?

The success of technology in the K–12 world is strongly influenced by the experiences and preparation students have with technology in their higher education programs and activities. If the program model is innovative and workable and makes effective use of technology, it will greatly impact how educators bring technology to their classrooms in the K–12 world.

In looking at higher education's response, or lack of it, to the prospect of "technologizing" instructional programs and their delivery, we can identify two distinct yet related areas: (1) the general attitude among college and university faculty to utilize technology in their course preparation and delivery and (2) the issue of teacher preparation, the prime entry point for technology to be understood and used in the K–12 classrooms.

The Machiavelli quote at the beginning of the chapter aptly describes higher education as it confronts the challenge of technology. There is an "old order" that has done well in living up to the traditions and culture of entrenched systems and values and in effect represents an enemy to this set of innovations represented by technology. The old order and lukewarm defenders resist taking full advantage of the benefits technology can bring to educational programs and activities.

UTILIZING TECHNOLOGY IN COURSE PREPARATION AND DELIVERY

Higher education (including community colleges, four-year colleges, universities, and adult education programs) is facing two issues: low enthusiasm for the use of technology in course development and delivery and a lack of understanding about the way it should be used to reshape educational programs.

Begun in 1990, the *Campus Computing Survey* (www.campus computing.net) is the largest continuing study of information technology in American higher education. This annual survey focuses on the use of computing and information technology in higher education. In the 2003 report Kenneth Green, founding director, comments that he has found an increasing use of technology to support instruction and the increasing role of course and learning management software. However, "few campuses provide recognition and reward for faculty efforts at instructional integration . . . in the their review and promotion process" (p. 7). This lack of recognition and reward are an indication of the struggle technology still faces to become enthusiastically accepted in course development and delivery in higher education.

Reluctance to utilize technology in course preparation and delivery remains very strong. There is an influx of people who grew up with technology and who are increasingly using it to support instruction, but they are still a minority of the faculty. The largest percentage of faculty are those who grew up in what Arlene Krebs (director of the wireless education and technology center at California State University–Monterey Bay) refers to as the "typewriter generation."

What are the issues, fears, and concerns—the reluctance factors—that lie behind the typewriter generation's unwillingness to use technology in college and university classrooms and lecture halls?

What's behind the Reluctance Factors?

The following is not intended to be a complete listing of reasons to resist the use of technology in higher education but does provide a general understanding of the key factors influencing this reluctance:

- Reluctance to change
- A culture that values independent iconoclasts
- Cost of ownership, utilization, and increased workload (with increased use of technology)
- Time and energy
- Role of faculty: Vulcan mind melder, creators of knowledge, or . . .
- Evidence of success
- Accountability, recognition, and reward for technological innovation and utilization

Reluctance to Change

> Nobody likes change except wet babies.
>
> —Allan Dobrin, senior vice chancellor and chief operating
> officer, City University of New York

It is human nature to resist change. In an interview Allan Dobrin provided a cogent summation about change in higher education:

> In every organization people resist change, it is just a human quality. Even change agents, whose job is to help others change, don't like to make personal change. So if something foreign, such as technology comes into people's lives, it is natural for them not to want to use it, they want to do things like they did before.

In the case of businesses, people had no choice, if you didn't make change you would go out of business. Educators as a rule are not risk takers (entrepreneurs are more likely to be a risk taker). So in college and universities there is a risk adverse group.

Higher education is one of the oldest institutions in society (along with the Catholic church) and we have a tradition of avoiding change. When you introduce technology, nothing bad happens to you if you don't use the new tools available to you, so there is no reason to use them. The result is an inertia, a resistance to change. In elementary schools, there is also no negative consequence if you do not use technology, and that is at the heart of why it doesn't happen.

A Culture That Values "Independent Iconoclasts"

The story is told that when General Eisenhower became the president of Columbia University, he was discussing the types of changes he would like to make in how the university was run. One of his staff looked at Eisenhower and commented, "You have to understand, general, that faculty ARE the university."

An important part of the culture of higher education that is valued and perpetuated by faculty is the right to be independent iconoclasts (a term we first heard from Ron Spalter of City University of New York). Lev Gonick, vice president for information technology services and chief information officer at Case Western Reserve University, in a talk he gave, commented that trying to bring a major change, such as the increasing and cooperative use of technology, to higher education is like trying to herd cats. He showed a wonderful commercial for a high-tech company to illustrate his point; cowboys are trying to bring a herd of cats into town, and they are discussing the "satisfaction" they get from their work, as they tend to the various scratches and wounds they received from the roundup. The question becomes how to "round up" the faculty, so they agree to use new technology in their work.

Cost of Ownership, Utilization, and Increased Workload (with Increased Use of Technology)

The cost of ownership is a major concern, not just in terms of the purchasing cost of software and hardware (including upgrades and issues such as software bugs). Other costs include the costs of professional development, support services, and licensing of products.

For example, the cost of support services has been very high, including the cost of personnel to "hand hold" staff as they bring technology into their classrooms, handling the technical issues and concerns. As costs come down it is easier and less expensive to hire support personnel, and the savings allow more money to be spent on professional development and instructional design issues and needs.

Online Courses: A Case in Point

In discussing the cost of implementing online courses, Ron Spalter, the City University of New York deputy chief operating officer responsible for developing and deploying campuswide information system applications and infrastructures, commented,

> Online classes in higher education, under traditional arrangements, are due to fail because when moving a course online, the cost/benefit ratio suffers.
>
> The instructor must respond to e-mail, oversee online chat rooms and discussion groups, and so on; so call time has to be decreased because he can't spend as much time as needed as he is still stuck in the Carnegie Unit [a measure of the number of hours a student had studied discrete subjects, the Carnegie unit is a measure of exposure to teaching]. If faculty is responsible for teaching 15 Carnegie hours per week per semester (easily met with classroom instruction), the issue is how does that equate to online education programs.

Spalter further commented, "We will lose money for every online class we offer, because faculty will generally not work harder or longer for the same pay, they are not willing to trade their time in front of the room for all the time that will be required being online."

For online education to be successful at the higher education level a different model not limited to Carnegie hours is required. Other higher education organizations, such as the University of Phoenix Online, have created programs not limited to Carnegie hours.

Time and Energy

Faculty who are not technologically inclined are not eager to put in the time and energy required to learn to use the technology. A faculty member often has to make a decision: Do I invest my time in getting my technology skills up to the certainty I need or do I write and publish journal articles to the standard needed for attaining tenure.

Investing time to build a catalog of technology-derived courses and materials will ultimately save time in the delivery of courses. For example, updating courses is easy with the click of a mouse, but many don't want to change—they don't want to reinvent themselves and have done well in the old order of things.

It takes more time to prepare a course that is designed using various technological tools, resources, and approaches, such as course management systems. Arlene Krebs, director of the Wireless Education and Technology Center at California State University–Monterey Bay commented on three stages of evolution for teaching with technology: "It generally takes three times teaching with a learning management system before one can master it: the first time is basically converting a paper-and-pencil course into online text; the second time you need to revise and enhance the course, using more multimedia elements; the third time the course is delivered, you master the interactive component of the course."

There is also the issue of who owns the intellectual property: if a faculty member creates a course for her class using innovative ideas and technology, do the rights to the content of the course belong to the faculty member or the university? (The decision as to who owns the property is left to each school's determination.)

Some faculty looked at the entrepreneurial opportunities presented by technology, thinking they could "cash in" on the material and course(s) they developed. However, with programs (e.g., MIT) opening their course materials to anyone who wants to use them, as well as the open source movement, the idea of making a lot of money from courses faculty develop has generally been dispelled. ("Open source" refers to a program in which the source code is available to the general public for use and/or modification from its original design free of charge.)

No or Minimal Impetus for Professional Development

Higher education, as a rule, does not organize professional development for faculty, though there is support for attending professional conferences or delivering a paper. Though there is a trend toward offering instruction in using pedagogical tools, it is a voluntary, please-come-if-and-when-you-can approach.

Role of Faculty: Vulcan Mind Melders, or Creators of Knowledge, or . . .

Father Guido Sarducci is a fictional character created by comedian Don Novello. He has a classic routine entitled "The Five-Minute University" in which he offers people a college education for $20 that takes five minutes to complete. His college program consists of learning what the average college student remembers after five years of leaving college. For example, his class on economics consists in memorizing the key concept of supply and demand (he has thought about opening a law school, if the student has a minute).

How faculty members view the legacy they want to leave with their students greatly impacts how and what they teach. Some want students to just show what they remember by the end of the term so that their grade can be determined (students view content as relevant only if it appears on the final exam), i.e., a sort of Vulcan mind meld (a reference from the TV show *Star Trek* where Spock touched his fingertips to someone's temples so that he and the other person could immediately read each other's thoughts). The persons believing in this model will, for the most part, be the sage on the stage who expects students to repeat their thoughts back to them; they may use some technology but only as a visual textbook. More than likely they will teach from the "typewriter-age" mentality, with minimal interest in and use of technology.

Facilitators and Filters

George Otte, director of instruction technology at City University of New York, discusses the role of faculty in the classroom as that of a facilitator and intermediary. He comments, "A teacher's critical role is to help each student understand what to do with the information so it becomes applied. The key point is to take information and turn it into knowledge, by application, practice and interaction." He further explains why the teacher needs to be an intermediary: "Now students see so much data, they look to the teacher to be the intermediary, to help decide what are good sources of information and good information. In essence the teacher becomes a filter."

The majority of students do research on the Web, but the data isn't vetted and students all too often assume it is the truth; they need to develop the ability to evaluate data. Though faculty may be reluctant entrants into the use of technology, like it or not, this role of faculty as facilitators and filters is essential to ensure their students understand, correctly evaluate, and use correct data and sources.

Evidence of Success

The film *Jerry McGuire* contains a phrase that has become part of the American vernacular, "Show me the money." Many are asking the question about the use of technology with the question, Show me the evidence of success [in utilizing technology in higher education course delivery and development].

Kenneth Green commented in an article he wrote entitled "To Epiphany—and Beyond!" (2004),

> Yes, technology—from film and television to online content and interactive simulations—can aid and enhance instruction and learning. But we do not have a clear definition for instructional productivity or precise methods to measure student learning and outcomes. At the classroom, program, and institutional level, we do not have firm definitions and consistent measures to assess what we do with IT resources or the impact of institutional IT investments and deployment efforts.
>
> So while we may not be able to define academic productivity, we know it when we see it or, more precisely, when we *experience* it. In other words, we have evidence by epiphany. Which innovations make a difference in teaching and learning and the need to understand the connection between educational computing, learning, and teaching.

Many educators are still not willing to accept "evidence by epiphany."

Accountability, Recognition, and Reward
for Developing Courses with Technology

Allan Dobrin commented, "For technology to be more broadly implemented in higher education organizations, you have to make people more comfortable with change, as well as move the educational environment to where educators are held more accountable. You would also need to get a system of rewards for student's performance, this will motivate educators to find tools to help them perform better, and lead to greater integration of technology."

Few higher education organizations offer a major reward or acknowledgment in terms of tenure for a faculty member who adopts and adapts technology in creating innovative classroom activities (service and scholarship are still the main considerations).

Kenneth Green (2004) commented, "This decade may be marked by efforts to make institutions accountable for the continuing (and rising) investment in IT [information technology]. Inquiring minds—board members and public officials, parents, and even some faculty—will focus on two questions: (1) Why don't faculty do more with technology? and (2) Why don't colleges and universities make better use of information technology in campus operations and services? As we enter the third decade of the 'computer revolution' in higher education, these seem like fair, timely, and, yes, admittedly difficult questions that we in the campus community will have to address."

What Does This All Mean?

Even though technology has strong implications for improving the development and delivery of instructional programs and classes, there is a strong reluctance factor at work in higher education concerning its use. There are significant efforts under way, however, to increase the level of enthusiasm and knowledge base for these new digital resources to be used in our universities.

Organizations such as EDUCAUSE (whose goal is to transform higher education through the use of information technology) and the League for Innovation in the Community College (committed to improving community colleges through innovation, experimentation, and institutional transformation) have been very effective in bringing an increased understanding about the value and use of technology in higher education.

The universities mentioned in this chapter—CUNY (City University of New York), Case Western Reserve University, California State

University–Monterey Bay—are examples of organizations that are creating innovative, leading edge programs.

There is a saying, Open your arms to change but don't let go of your values. The strength and impact of a university is in large measure built on the magnificence of its faculty. Higher education faces the challenge, as technology assumes a more prominent position in learning and instruction, of helping the "independent iconoclasts" understand how the utilization of technology will enhance their goals. Faculty will expand their use of technology when they observe that their educational and professional values are more fulfilled and they are rewarded by the application of technology.

TEACHER PREPARATION AND TECHNOLOGY

The university school of education, the teacher preparation mill, is the part of the higher education world where a great deal can be accomplished in changing the direction of K–12 education. Unfortunately, this potential is rarely realized.

Year in, year out, undergraduates leave the university prepared for their first teaching experiences. At present, they rarely receive workable preparation in the use of technology to support teaching and learning and what little professional development they do receive comes from the school system they end up working with. Yet school districts have little time, money, or resources to use in making up for this deficit. The most likely current scenario is that the teacher who begins a career without preparation in using technology will simply avoid it.

When schools and districts offer in-service training in the use of technology, it is usually too little to be of much use. Teachers don't have time to participate in much training and career development; they are simply too busy in their classrooms with their students. The amount of reflection on the nature of technology and its import, the number of models and examples that need to be absorbed in order to develop the instincts needed to reconceive pedagogical approaches that take advantage of the new resources, is quite extensive.

This should not be confused with deep training to master complex technology skills. It has more to do with understanding how the technology has restructured and recontextualized the goals and logistics of learning, and knowing the implications of this for teaching. Consequently, the schools of education are by far the best entry point.

That new teachers must take their place in the profession prepared in the light of the existence of powerful new technologies is no idle suggestion. At this point in time, establishing the proper role for technology in education is mission critical. No contemporary institution can buck the tide of human intellectual evolution by avoiding the tools that shape it. And there is no better place where this can be changed than the place where our teachers are produced.

Interview with Rose Reissman

Rose Reissman has been involved as a teacher educator and adjunct/ associate professor of higher education for more than eighteen years, including involvements at Columbia University and Long Island University, as well a the Hunter College and CUNY higher education programs.

Her comments below are based on her personal experiences and observations through her distinguished career.

RR: To put it bluntly there is a disconnect between higher education teacher education programs, and I have witnessed a broad spectrum of these, and the actual classroom educators' access to technology, ability to integrate technology, and introduction to classroom-specific, curriculum-connected technology expressions. Sad to say, what I've witnessed over my many years of working in graduate teacher education, and it's only within the last two years that I've actually been allowed, as a so-called literacy English literature expert, to actually integrate technology myself.

Most teacher education programs have a course called Ed Tech, meaning that these are pure technology courses. These courses were originally designed in the 1980s and 1990s as pure technology training or integration courses . . . they involve the participants being introduced to a set of software and technology applications which have been selected by their instructors (for the most part they are not professors). These are educational technology experts who have not even taught in the schools. They introduce software programs they like, which are often disconnected from any practical application in the school. Or they show the participants how to use products that can be used for the school, such as Inspiration, PowerPoint, various other programs, but *not* in a way that connects to the curriculum that the participating student educators are using or will be using in the schools.

Mark: Is it the lack of vision of the dean, and others in the education department that causes them to view technology as a novelty and not a prime tool essential for teaching?

RR: Basically, it's not that the deans don't have vision, but a dean or someone who heads these programs comes from a Literacy background, i.e., has been a content professor in the graduate education department and is many, many years removed from classroom teaching, if they taught in the classroom at all.

Most of those individuals I've encountered running education departments, most likely did not teach in an urban inner-city setting and are very disconnected from technology. They are content based and they see technology as a frill.

So, they hire people who generally do not have a ranking, or they belong to the math, science, technology connection. Ultimately, they want to make sure that their lab facility is used, and that their students feel that they are being given technology.

Mark: What is very disturbing about this is that school systems depend on teaching schools to provide qualified, prepared, entry-level teachers; it looks like the school system, the consumer, is doing more to prepare the teachers to use technology than the higher education qualifying institution is.

RR: It's sad to say, but that's true. Many of these graduate schools have adopted schools within districts as their lab schools or districts with whom they partner on grants, and where their student teachers do their internships, The irony is that they should draw on the technology, using strengths of those schools by having the full-time tenured professors visit these schools to inform themselves about the use of technology. And then fabric into their courses these valuable models of technology use.

I have become fascinated with technology and I have been using technology resources in the courses I teach, be they in literacy or social studies, involving analysis of Web resources and the development of "webliographies," for instance.

Mark: So what can we do about this situation? You are a fairly recent technology convert, having become enchanted with technology within the past year or so. Over the decades you have prepared teachers and prepared them well, but within an almost exclusively print context. Now, how will you use the wonderful new possibilities with technology that you see?

RR: I think that my case illuminates a larger implication for graduate professors.

Number one, I think that having the technology professor who is not an education professor but who is proficient with the technology, familiar with software, etc., is not a good thing.

The university where I teach has presented a good model with its computer lab. It allows all of the professors to take their students into the lab to enable them to integrate some technology into their courses. We could use more of this at other schools. Also, the professors and adjuncts need to have the opportunity to attend seminars and training in the use and the integration of technology into their disciplines, something that is not currently offered. I doubt that this would be very expensive, and money is not the prime reason it doesn't happen.

The logical next step would be for these professors to include a technology requirement for their course. This is especially important for teachers in training. It is common for such students to have to prepare a personal portfolio and that one section of this portfolio should address the teacher's use of technology. Although this is not currently stressed, it ought to be. (2003)

Reissman's experience is typical of faculty who teach education majors in our schools of education. Little wonder, therefore, that the shift to technology-supported education isn't happening in our public schools, considering the short shrift it gets in higher education.

Schools of education inform and guide the K–12 world. Their indifference is a double misfortune because in modeling the use of technology for students who are preparing to become teachers, schools would learn to use it to impact the programs offered in all majors. It would appear that without the world of higher education taking a lead role, the adoption of instructional technology is an agenda that will not be realized soon.

FINAL WORD: PROGRESS WITH CHANGE

Questions that need to be asked include the following: How are the typewriter-age people going to be merged into the information age in higher education? How can this be done in spite of the independent iconoclasts—those who have done well under the old order and are reluctant to change? Do we wait until the typewriter-age people leave the profession or are there actions we can take now?

Jack Welch, former General Electric CEO, commented, "The end is near, when changes outside a system dwarf adaptations inside it." Some predict the eventual demise of higher education as we know it today, in large measure because of the possibilities that technology brings. Online educational programs and developments such as MIT's opening course content for use by nonstudents are prime examples of the changes taking place. All aspects of our culture are being broadly affected by the burgeoning use of technology; higher education must keep pace and set the example of how to creatively and insightfully implement technology.

The Saudi Arabian government reportedly developed a slogan to celebrate the sixtieth anniversary of the kingdom: Sixty years of progress, without change. For higher education to flourish, faculty must make "progress with change" in how they address instruction in the age of technology, or students will increasingly find their needs being met by places other than higher education.

CHAPTER 8

Dream Big

Never doubt that a small group of thoughtful, committed citizens can change the world. Indeed, it's the only thing that ever has.

—Margaret Mead

> What needs to be done to bring the awesome power of technology into the world of education? Who can help and how?

TECH TO GO: A TIPPING POINT

In November 2002, the third annual Tech to Go conference was held in New York City. This free conference drew over a thousand teachers who were willing to spend a Saturday, a day off, to obtain professional development in the use of classroom technology. Luring teachers to Saturday workshops, even when they are paid for their time, is difficult. Tech to Go, however, offered no remuneration.

For three years teachers attended this conference in droves. They came to learn how to use the computers that had been placed in their classrooms for the benefit of their students. Many believe that Tech to Go produced far better results in preparing teachers in this area than many other opportunities made available either through time off from work or for overtime pay.

Those who attended accepted the challenge of an event that tapped into their higher calling as teachers. They saw attending Tech to Go as an opportunity to change the world within their classroom in a small yet profound way. The first year of the event, it was given the descriptive subtitle "A Digital Woodstock," a moniker that reflected the organizers' intent to stage a "tipping point" event through which a movement would recognize itself. Over the years it became clear that this was precisely the type of folks who turned out, self-styled fifth columnists, workers within a massive bureaucracy who would grab any opportunity to reform negative conditions. Classroom technology represented such an opportunity.

The name Tech to Go refers to the stated context and promise of the conference. Its many dozens of workshops were organized around the principle of offering ready-to-go lessons and free resources—in hourlong sessions. This was exactly what teachers wanted. The poster announcing the conference promised that they would return to their classrooms the following Monday morning armed with a body of new things to do with their students, right away . . . Tech to Go. The popularity of this event demonstrates teachers' readiness to explore and embrace technology when it is prepared and presented to them properly.

IT'S TIME TO LOOK AT THINGS DIFFERENTLY

The struggle to bring technology into the education we offer our young people has been going on for over two decades. Many observers see a disturbing change in the trajectory of the instructional technology agenda. The hard-won momentum that instructional technology experienced for a number of years has slackened. Between the bad rap that it accrued from early missteps and the current back-to-basics focus in education, interest and confidence have been lost.

There are generally three basic approaches that can be taken to make major changes in a situation. More of something can be done, it can be done better, or it can be done differently. The examples of technology use cited earlier in this book indicate that doing something better is not what's needed. We've included examples aplenty of excellence in technology use. Nor is there much opportunity to do more of what has been done already. Perhaps it is time to do things differently.

INTEGRATION IS TECHNOLOGY CALLING ATTENTION
TO ITSELF

For many years "technology integration" has been a high-profile goal in the educational community. That schools should acquire and integrate technology into the instructional program was a given. Lately, though, with the push for a back-to-basics, literacy- and math-focused program, as well as the passing of the technology novelty factor, integration is no longer often cited as a goal.

This is a negative development with a silver lining. Integration is not a concept that aids the agenda in the long run. It has accrued a connotation of something extremely hard to do and almost impossible to achieve. And it involves the struggle for an undefined goal. Integration is technology calling attention to itself, something that makes it a distraction, not an asset. We would be wise to revise the language associated with instructional technology.

It would be far better for educators to demand *preintegrated* technology-based resources. As noted earlier, software is needed that functions as a prime instructional resource, not an ancillary one. Once software is considered to represent core, mission-critical math or science or social studies materials, not "technology" items, the institution of school will see technology as mainstream.

Software need not compete with the books currently used. It can be developed by the same publishers to address the same needs and purpose, with both resources working toward a synergy. Eventually each resource will assume its proper role in a holistic environment. Such resources must be easy to use. We know from deep experience already that software can function easily for educators, especially those who have only entry level technology skills: To read, reflect, follow directions, click the mouse, and so on, is all it takes to get started. Publishers will get the idea once the ball starts rolling and keep simplifying and expanding their offerings.

Class websites provide a good example of a tech-to-go resource awaiting mass adoption. While producing the traditional website requires learning, there are other approaches. Teachers and students can have a Web presence without acquiring specialized authoring software, paying for hosting service, or learning the intricacies of FTPing files to a remote server. Free and effortless sites are available from groups like Yahoo! Geocities. Such sites can be set up in less than an hour, offer great possibilities for teaching, and require nothing more than a standard Web browser to access.

Cliff Stoll gets it right in his book *High Tech Heretic* in the chapter entitled "Loony for Laptops." Technology-based instructional programs that put most attention on the technology itself—acquiring, training to use, maintaining, and so on—are not destined to provide the models of success needed to bring about a definitive shift in attitude and behavior among educators. There are inexpensive, easy-to-use, nearly transparent technologies that the world of education ought to be looking at.

THE FIX

So, what's the fix . . . how do we get back online and reconnect education to the power of technology?

The most important thing to understand is that a change in attitudes and understandings is far more important than action items and expenditures of funds. With the correct mind-set, the rest of it will fall into place.

NECESSARY CORE UNDERSTANDINGS
AND ATTITUDES TO ADOPT

We are at a crossroads. In a sense, we may be looking at education's digital last chance for success in the new age of technology and information revolution. The crucial shift in understanding is to acknowledge that there is no choice in bringing technology into education. The human race has gone too far down the path of technology adoption and dependence to avoid its profound influence on school and the other principal manifestations of education, such as educational television and entertainment; books, magazines, and newspapers for young people; and educational games and toys. It *will* insert itself in education as it has in every other institution. The question is, do we want to direct a sensible, positive "technologizing" of the institution of education, or do we want to let technology show up and assert itself, catch as catch can?

Books, our purest icon of the value of literacy, are profoundly affected by technology. Books and technology now go hand in hand and we must understand and embrace that. We are not helping our young people develop as literate beings by keeping them from technology in a desperate attempt to get them to appreciate the book. Rejecting today's digital technologies as a prime resource for education, particularly in the areas of literacy and literacy across the curriculum, is shortsighted and will only promote the irrelevance of our schools. Computers will never replace good teachers.

The best approach for technology use in education is to have teachers mediate the technology for and with their students. We cannot avoid this scenario any more than we can avoid having technology in the classroom.

Above all, we need to start seeing technology as something that is easy to use. The skills involved are not difficult to master. The concepts involved in the use of technology as an instructional resource are not difficult to comprehend either. Beyond the crucial aspect of preparing ourselves with the appropriate mind-set, there are some real things we can and should do.

With a few notable exceptions, the purveyors of hardware have not sufficiently provided instructional content and resources. It should become an expectation that manufacturers and vendors do so. In the long run, getting their customers to use what they have purchased, and use it well, is in the manufacturers' best interests. We are currently hitting a wall, a point at which potential purchasers are becoming increasingly doubtful about the unproven claims for technology. They doubt that simply putting information technology in the hands of students and teachers will enable them to find their way to the content they need.

The type of resource that teachers and students demand is crucial. The Tech to Go approach will precipitate the greatest results and change in the world of education: easy to use, easy to benefit from, trouble free; the Read, Write, Think website is a good example. More resources like this will result in greater utilization and greater demand for more of the same in an ongoing cycle of success.

There is a plethora of appropriate, effective, easy-to-use material and resources on the Web. Few teachers, however, know that it is there or know how to find it. It sits in countless websites, all of which purport to offer the world unique gems. Notable among these are the websites of the various discipline-oriented professional teacher organizations, for instance, the National Council of Teachers of Math. *What is needed is a metasite, a single interface through which all of this material can be located, analyzed, compared, and accessed.*

Mandating the use of technology will not work. Many of the areas of education that professionals and the public currently consider failing or troubled involve mandates that are not met or are met with no resultant satisfaction. Technology is part and parcel of out-of-the-box thinking; resorting to mandates, a prime example of thinking inside the box, will not make it work.

Who should be involved in promoting the use of technology in our schools? Not instructional technologists, at least not exclusively! The value of the technology lies in its role as a support and enhancement for teaching and learning in the subject areas. Consequently, leaders in the areas of language arts, math, science, and so on, must take responsibility to see to it that technology is tapped to further learning in these areas. Until this happens, very little technology will be tapped to improve education, at least not in schools!

ACTION ITEMS

Now that we have a core understanding about what is at stake, there are things that must be done in order to move the agenda forward. There are action items for all players in the game of instructional technology and in the end they must all participate in order for progress to be made. The following is a list of them organized by player.

School District Administration

School district administrators are probably the linchpin to moving the agenda forward. Through their experienced understanding and strategically adept actions, much can be done. However, if this group of key players abdicates its responsibility, it is likely that teachers will take matters into their own hands and attempt to move the agenda forward through fifth-column actions of their own. This was evidenced by Tech to Go. Administrators should take the following steps:

1. Charge the instructional leaders of the district (language arts, math, science, etc., all those responsible for supervising and providing professional development in these areas) with exploring and adopting technology to support teaching and learning in those areas. They may get support from the district's instructional technology staff, but as long as this responsibility is fully given over to instructional technologists, the rift between the jurisdictions of the two will defeat attempts to bring technology into the subject areas, which is the true goal.
2. Establish an expectation among teacher preparation schools and potential teacher hires that familiarity with technology and how it may be used to support instruction is a criterion for employment in the district.
3. Establish an expectation among school district instructional technology staff that understanding instruction must become part of their skill set. Instructional technologists must understand the purposes for which technology is to be used, as well as the equipment.
4. In shopping for software, examine free resources first. By letting publishers know that the district will not pay for things that can be acquired free, it will be redirecting the publisher to develop other, more elaborate items. In the end, the outcome will be a better set of materials available to schools.
5. Encourage print publishers to provide free software to complement text and other print materials that they sell. In this way, traditional, text-driven schools will not face the seemingly overwhelming job of figuring out how to align their new technology programs to the print materials they depend on for the bulk of their program. This should appeal to print publishers because it will allow them to enter the field of software publishing, something they want to do anyway but in many cases have not found a rationale to support.

State Education Departments

First, list and review free Web-based resources for teachers on the state's education portal. Establish a statewide listserv for all teachers to inform them about updates as new resources come out. Second, formalize the licensing of district-level instructional technology administrators, as well as school-based technology teachers, by establishing license areas for these two types of positions.

Teachers

Familiarize themselves with available teaching resources on the Web. Encourage students to use technology for research, writing, and report projects. See the section below entitled "Essential Resources for Jump-Starting Teacher Technology Use."

School Principals and Assistant Principals

Establish a school club that will teach youngsters how to do simple repairs and maintenance on the school's technology equipment and enable them to function as technology advisers to teachers as they expand their understanding and skill in the use of technology for teaching and learning.

Software Publishers

First, reconfigure the packaging of software so that schoolwide or districtwide purchases are not a requirement of purchasing software. Encouraging schools to pay for only the software they use will eliminate some of the cost-driven disincentives to technology use, create goodwill, and give the company's development department accurate feedback about what is needed and wanted.

Second, give free access to some content offerings as a way of familiarizing teachers with them and winning teachers over to their use. Develop software for sale that interfaces with free content and extends it.

Hardware Manufacturers

Provide free content to support the use of the hardware produced and sold. This content should not be directed exclusively at the long-term integration approach to use that requires extensive professional development. Teachers need Tech to Go–type resources that do not require the extensive learning of tech skills or the labor-intensive creation of their own materials.

Universities

Make deep understanding of technology a part of teacher preparation. Use technology to deliver coursework for all offerings so that instructional technology is modeled across the board.

ESSENTIALS RESOURCES FOR JUMP-STARTING TEACHER TECHNOLOGY USE

Following is a list of Web-based resources that will illustrate the possibilities of technology to teachers who are new to its use. They will inspire and reinvigorate teaching careers, an aspect of technology adoption not often spoken of but one of its prime potentials. Any such list is subjective and is fated to be outdated as soon as it is created. However, these are "killer" resources and will deliver as promised. Newbies will undoubtedly find others on their own. This is as it should be.

1. MarcoPolo Internet Content for the Classroom (www.marcopolo-education.org/index.aspx). Easy to understand and use, this site is chock full of Tech to Go. There are materials here for every subject and every level. Nothing about technology need be learned. Teachers can simply tap into powerful resources and use them right away.

2. International Society for Technology in Education (www.iste.org). A broad potpourri of resources and background information is presented here, the site of the world's leading professional organization for the use of technology in education.

3. ALI (Apple Learning Interchange) (ali.apple.com/ali/resources .shtml). A rich collection of free resources created by school-based practitioners and assembled by Apple Computer. There are teaching practices and lesson ideas, examples of projects, materials on leadership and professional growth, and so on. As might be expected of Apple, there is a decided tilt toward the use of multimedia, which is made easy.

4. Scholastic (www.scholastic.com). One of the oldest and best-known publishers of books for young people. Its website is devoted to the needs of teachers and is enriched with many resources beyond titles for sale. The site is easy to use and

nontechnology using teachers need only acquire the most basic tech skills and understandings in order to take advantage of its broad array of rich resources. Literacy is a major component of the site. Among the many free offerings are activities that employ the Internet to put youngsters in touch with authors with whom they can exchange ideas.

5. Kathy Schrock (school.discovery.com/schrockguide). The first and last word on where to find and how to use content on the Web. Hundreds and hundreds of content-bearing sites are indexed by subject as well as alphabetically. A raft of user-friendly search engines help the content-hungry teacher find still more. There is also an array of teacher resources to support teachers in the use of Web content.

6. *THE Journal* (www.thejournal.com). *Technology Horizons in Education.* For a number of years this print and online magazine, as well as related services, has informed educators about developments in the use of technology for education. The journal covers educational practices, research, and trends. It offers product reviews and highlights and gives insightful editorials on the continually evolving field of instructional technology. The online magazine has an extensive archive of back articles that form a searchable and significant slice of technology knowledge for education.

7. Technology and Learning (www.techlearning.com). This site offers an online version of the popular magazine (by the same name) for educators as well as resources and opportunities to learn about technology for learning. The site is loaded with tips about how to use, manage, and teach with and about technology for the classroom. It provides insight into education hot issues from the perspective of a tech-using educator. This site also offers listings and reviews of new products as well as notices about grants, awards, and other opportunities for teachers and schools.

8. HPRC (High Plains Regional Technology in Education Consortium) (www.hprtec.org). Starting in 1995, regional consortia were created by the U.S. Department of Education as a first step toward forming a national system of service providers. These consortia, known as R-TECs (regional technology in education

consortia), now include consortia in the Appalachian, High Plains, Mid-Atlantic, North Central, Northeast and the Islands, Pacific, South Central, Southeast, and Southwest regions. All are gold mines of information and resources. The High Plains regions website is particularly enticing for teachers getting themselves up to speed on the use of technology. The site has resources for teachers as well as activities for students. There are tools, tutorials, and content here, some of it created by students as well as educators.

9. ENC (Eisenhower National Clearinghouse) (www.enc.org). The Eisenhower National Clearinghouse for Mathematics and Science Education (ENC) is located at Ohio State University and is funded through a contract with the U.S. Department of Education. Its mission is to identify effective curriculum resources, create high-quality professional development materials, and disseminate useful information and products to improve K–12 mathematics and science teaching and learning. A visit to the site will show the close alignment between instructional technology and these goals. The rich, extensive online resources this site offers represent a highly effective realization of that mission. Nonmath or science educators will obtain insight into what is possible for education through the use of technology by visiting, observing, and reflecting.

10. NASA Education Enterprise (http://education.nasa.gov/home/index.html). A mother lode of resources organized into the following categories: kids, students, educators, and education news. And that's just the tip of the iceberg. Content, Web links, multimedia resources, news and articles, ask the expert, and much more. This free site will hold the distinction of science education's "killer app" far into the foreseeable future. While this material is overtly science, literacy and social studies curriculum connections abound.

FINAL WORD: DREAMING BIG: GOING FOR THE CHEESE

Beyond the action items enumerated above, which take advantage of existing, well-established structures, a few strategic tipping point phenomena may persuade mainstream education to finally embrace technology. Encouragingly, technology offers opportunities to create opportunities for technology.

NetDay, an organization that conducts its initiatives through a website, recently rallied students across vast distances in a single unified project. The online report of this program states, "The first Speak Up Day for Students, held in October 2003, produced the first ever large scale report of student voices and views. NetDay encourages students to use the surveys and the data to engage in local discussions to improve education in their communities. What can you do now?"

The event had students in 3,000 schools discussing and participating in a mass survey of data and opinion on the value of technology for youngsters. Over 200,000 surveys were completed and submitted by youngsters in a little over a week!

The organization, as follow-up, encourages students to recruit teachers to participate in the Speak Up Day for Teachers event, a similar effort—to share results with their local decision makers so that the movement for technology adoption as well as the tech status of their school are known—and to host focus groups to reflect on these experiences and plan for future action.

The success of this first effort is remarkable and is due to the use of the modest but ubiquitous technology of the World Wide Web. Furthermore, it points to the huge unmet need as the institution of education continues to muddle along ignoring the pressing desire for appropriate technology adoption of its constituents. If the powers in charge of the school institution don't heed the call, then a grassroots movement in the making will fill the gap.

In May 2004 another event took place that literally redefined the way that education can be structured and delivered. Megaconference Jr. (http://megaconferencejr.cciu.org/call.htm) was held in cyberspace and thousands of youngsters from around the world attended. This event took advantage of the more sophisticated types of technology that will be part of broad-based implementation in just a short while. The conference's online announcement and invitation stated, "Megaconference Jr. is a new project designed to give students in elementary and secondary schools around the world the opportunity to communicate, collaborate, and contribute to each other's learning in real time, using advanced multipoint video conferencing technology."

Among the many who answered the call for presentations were students from the Poi Ching School of Singapore, presenting on International Friendship Day; kids at the Eddy Elementary School in Mississippi, presenting their fourth grade wax museum project; youngsters from the Pegaso school in Catalonia, presenting "My Town Is Barcelona"; students from the Northland College Kapa Haka Group, New Zealand, presenting the Maori language; and many more.

These events clearly point to a very profound change that has taken place. A raft of barriers, including distance, time, and age, among others, have been rendered impotent by the new digital technologies. Youngsters use these to collaborate and share by spoken, written, and Web-published word, ideas that move and inspire them. There is a level of engagement and fascination with content and social learning rarely witnessed in today's traditional schools. Through all of this is seen student work that speaks to high levels of learning. This is not unique. This book has shown a great many similar examples of smaller scale that have been around for years. What's different are the numbers and the potential for even greater participation.

We are moving toward that event, that long sought tipping point happening that will push us irrevocably into a new reality. The indications of its coming are clear. We hope that educators will make themselves aware of this digital tidal wave about to engulf them and harness its power for the benefit of our youth.

CHAPTER 9

Eleven Ways Technology Reinvigorates Learning

MOTIVATION

George Bernard Shaw once said, "What we want is the child in pursuit of knowledge, not knowledge in pursuit of the child." Our current education crisis is largely due to the inability of educators to engage students—ensure they are in pursuit of knowledge. Technology impacts profoundly on this impasse. The availability of unlimited content through the Web can ensure that all students learn from material that relates to their personal interest. Today's youngsters are growing up in a digital media, telecommunications-driven, microprocessor-saturated environment that they find stimulating, satisfying, inspiring, and comfortable. By directing these technologies at the work of teaching and learning, educators can recapture the hearts and minds of their students.

RECONTEXTUALIZED LEARNING—AND THE CAPABILITY TO MAKE A REAL DIFFERENCE, RIGHT NOW

School reform and innovation in instruction are a constant in the educational landscape, yet many alternative approaches to instruction loom as unattainable logical next steps. Technology makes many of these now possible. For example, through the use of specialized software, youngsters can be engaged in activities that structure an experience for collaborative learners. Without this capability teachers in a traditional classroom are hard-pressed to manage student attention, movement, time, and performance and opt for whole class instruction. Technology is particularly useful, too, in creating opportunities for authentic activities in which youngsters do real things in the real world. E-mailing senior citizens or tracking stock prices as they manage an investment portfolio are good examples. Project-based learning is often made possible through the use of technology, as are activities that involve higher order thinking skills, involving youngsters in framing questions and solving problems as they construct knowledge for themselves.

INDIVIDUALIZED AND CUSTOMIZED INSTRUCTION

Teachers of the traditional class of thirty-plus students most typically deliver a single lesson to that class. This is done for purely practical reasons even though individualized and customized lessons are often an elusive ideal. Technology offers new opportunities to achieve this unrealized goal. Much instructional software has been produced for this purpose. The vast scanning, analyzing, and processing capability of computers allows teachers to provide content that periodically requires students to respond to questions that probe for understanding and learning. Instant grading of responses guides the computer as it either sends the student on to material beyond what has been learned or redirects them to material to be reviewed until the goal is achieved. The content provided to each student can be tailored to each student's needs, interests, and purposes according to his or her profile.

IMPROVED WRITING THROUGH A
TECHNOLOGY-FACILITATED WRITING PROCESS

Writing is a skill that is essential to success in all fields of study and professional practice. For decades, educators have struggled to improve the level of learning in this area. Employers, too, are dissatisfied with the level of writing ability exhibited by the workforce. Word processing, graphic organizer, and content specific software facilitate the process of learning to write. They guide the creation of outlines; eliminate the drudgery of rewriting numerous copies of drafts; offer support with the potential distractions of problems in spelling, grammar, and format; allow the writer to easily retain and compare various versions of his work; facilitate the laborious process of searching and replacing words, names, and phrases; and allow the writer to produce a professional, finished-looking product. The improvement of writing is a dynamic that relates to all of the items listed below.

STUDENT PUBLISHING

Educators have long considered "publishing" to be an essential and final phase in the writing process. Before the advent of desktop digital technology, they rarely had the capacity to do more than have students produce a single, handwritten copy to be pinned to a bulletin board or affixed to the refrigerator door with a magnet. The democratization of media through the ubiquitous presence of common office technology allows today's students, under the guidance of informed teachers, to produce much the same type of books, magazines, posters, and websites as the major players in the publishing industry. This type of publishing lends an authenticity and importance to student writing as youngsters create real content for real audiences. It is also a great way for students to demonstrate their competence and what they have produced, giving them a real purpose to ensure their work is up to the writing standards expected of published works.

RESEARCH

Research is another core skill and activity that has long frustrated educators. The logistics involved make it difficult; no matter how extensive the school's library, there simply isn't enough content available to support more than superficial research. Assigning research as homework or away from school activity is helpful in allowing the student greater access to content, but imposes the difficulty of time delay between assigning, researching, reporting, and reflecting on the research. The use of the World Wide Web and browser and search engine technology eliminate the limitations research activities have presented traditionally. Research can now be a powerful, dynamic, and exciting part of every student's experience. Of course this also increases the necessity for instruction in evaluating what is a good and credible source of information (previously, with exclusive reliance on school libraries, the information vetted was by librarians).

MODELING, ILLUSTRATING, SIMULATIONS

Reading, writing, and discussion are great—up to a point. Our current textbook-driven, chalkboard-enabled, one-teacher-to-thirty-students mode of instruction manages to tap just a small fraction of student potential for understanding. The trend to do away with labs, shops, and other enhanced learning environments in our troubled, back-to-basics, financially challenged schools hasn't helped. Through the use of software and websites, concepts are easily brought alive and students offered many opportunities to see and experience things from a different angle that can make all the difference. Animations, interactive online tools that require making choices to influence outcomes, video and sound clips, virtual reality simulations, and a raft of other items can put students in the driver's seat of a space shuttle, have the experience of working with dangerous chemicals or biologic elements, or see the outcome of their own urban engineering experiments. An important component of learning is to observe the reality of things for oneself (not just in the abstract words of textbooks), technology makes this possible as never before.

MULTIPLE INTELLIGENCES

Reading of texts and discussion, while the backbone of traditional schooling, are not *the* exclusive ways in which youngsters learn. Other "intelligences" are part of the human intellectual makeup, according to psychologist Howard Gardner. Gardner lists the following intelligences: linguistic, logical-mathematical, musical, spatial, bodily kinesthetic, interpersonal, intrapersonal, and naturalist. Not all minds are the same and individuals learn best when given the opportunity to exercise intelligences and combinations that are theirs. While the theory of multiple intelligences is widely accepted, taking advantage of it in traditional classrooms is quite difficult. Because technology makes bringing such a wide variety of possibilities into the educational experience possible, it can transform the classroom into a multiple intelligence–centered learning environment.

CONNECTING TO EXPERTS AND MENTORS

Through the advent of the Web and e-mail, contacting others has been revolutionized. Students now can be in touch with individuals closely associated with what they are studying. Interaction with authors, journalists, scientists, and politicians can now be part of the education our young people receive. This can be accomplished on an ongoing basis with online mentors giving youngsters feedback on their work and involving them in their projects. Apprenticeship, a mode of education that predates schooling and largely was lost because of it, can be resurrected. Online, students can once again learn from practitioners instead of "teachers." But they can be in touch with a far greater number and variety of such mentors than was the case traditionally and have their mentor experience mediated for them by their teachers, the best of both worlds.

ADAPTIVE AND ASSISTIVE TECHNOLOGY

There is sufficient advanced technology available now to allow physically, emotionally, and intellectually challenged students to participate in many more mainstream educational activities than ever before. Specialized keyboards allow the physically impaired to use a computer and take advantage of its educational benefits. Even those unable to use their arms or hands can use devices such as the head mouse, an alternate way to manipulate a graphic user interface. There are many devices that enable nonverbal students to communicate with teachers and peers. Special educators have discovered that various software programs provide a fertile environment in which autistic students can be better engaged and focused on learning activities. Technology provides limitless possibilities opportunities for meaningful learning and participation to those challenged by their needs.

LEVERAGING THE WORK OF OTHERS

With so much access to so much content, learning has taken new and important paths. Mirroring work in the real world, student activities include not just inventing new wheels but also acknowledging the wheels created by others and extending that work. By using the Web as a clearinghouse, youngsters from around the world can collaborate to produce products and understandings far beyond the traditional. Ensuring students have a heightened understanding of plagiarism and intellectual property is part and parcel of these changes.

Bibliography

Alliance for Childhood. *Fool's Gold: A Critical Look at Computers and Childhood.* www.allianceforchildhood.net.

Blaisdell, Bob. "Why Computers Have Not Saved the Classroom." *Christian Science Monitor,* October 14, 2003. www.csmonitor.com/2003/1014/p20s02-lecl.html.

Cuban, Larry. *Oversold and Underused.* Cambridge, MA: Harvard University Press, 2001.

Gerstner, L. V., Jr. Remarks to the meeting of the National Education Summit, Palisades, NY, October 9, 2001. www.ibm.com/lvg/1009.phtml.

Green, Kenneth. *The Campus Computing Survey,* 2003. http://www.campus computing.net.

———. "To Epiphany—and Beyond!" *Syllabus,* April 2004, p. 18.

Healy, Jane. *Failure to Connect: How Computers Affect Our Children's Mind for Better and Worse.* New York: Simon & Schuster, 1998.

Kaun, Karen. Interview by Mark Gura, October, 2003.

Learning for the Twenty-First Century: A Report and Mile Guide for 21st Century Skills. Washington, DC: Partnership for 21st Century Skills.

McKenzie, Jamie. "One Flew over the High School." *From Now On: Educational Technology Journal,* December 2003. www.fno.org/dec03/flickering .html.

National Commission on Excellence in Education. *A Nation at Risk: The Imperative for Educational Reform.* Washington, DC, 1983.

Net Day. *Speak Up Day 2003.* www.netday.org/speakupday2003_report.htm.

November, Alan. "Teaching Zack to Think." *High School Principal,* September 1998.

Oppenheimer, Todd. *The Flickering Mind: The False Promise of Technology in the Classroom and How Learning Can Be Saved.* New York: Random House, 2003.

Papert, Seymour. *The Children's Machine*. New York: Basic, 1993.

Perelman, Lewis J. *School's Out: Hyperlearning, the New Technology, and the End of Education*. New York: Morrow, 1992.

Reissman, Rose. Interview by Mark Gura, December, 2003.

Rukeyser, William. *Digital Divide* (2000). www.pbs.org/digitaldivide/class-voices.html.

Scott, Norm. Interview by Mark Gura, December 2003.

Stoll, Clifford. *High Tech Heretic: Why Computers Don't Belong in the Classroom and Other Reflections by a Computer Contrarian*. New York: Doubleday, 1999.

Suarez-Orozco, Marcelo, and Howard Gardner. "Educating Billy Wang for the World of Tomorrow." *Education Week,* October 22, 2003, 34, 44.

Washington, Thomas. "Weeding: A Lament for the Loss of Books." *Education Week,* December 3, 2003, 31.

Worsnop, Chris M. "A Taxonomy Is Not a Sequence: Losing Our Way in the Standards-Based Curriculum." *Education Week,* October 15, 2003, 36.

Index

About the Authors

Mark Gura has been an educator for over three decades. The former director of instructional technology for the NYC public school system, he is a thought leader in this emerging field. Currently working with Fordham University's Regional Educational Technology Center, Mr. Gura draws on his extensive background as a literacy, science, and arts teacher to promote the creative use of technology for teaching and learning. He is the coauthor of *Making Literacy Magic Happen—The Best of Learning & Leading with Technology on Language Arts*, an ISTE publication, and has done extensive work in preparing teachers to be effective instructors in the digital age, designing and implementing professional development for thousands of teachers. He writes regularly for *Converge Magazine* and the *New York Daily News* and consults on matters of education and instructional technology throughout the New York City area. Mr. Gura lives with his wife Maria in Teaneck, New Jersey, and can be contacted by email at: markgura@optonline.net.

Bernard Percy was editor in chief of the award-winning education and technology magazine *Converge* from 1998 to 2003 and has authored books on education. He has over thirty years of experience in education in public, private, and corporate environments, including fourteen years teaching in the New York City and Los Angeles public school systems. Percy has lectured on a variety of education issues in Russia, Japan, China, Canada, and Australia. He has served as a juror evaluating educational technology projects and programs for international competitions, including the Stockholm Challenge (Sweden) and the Global Junior Challenge (Italy).